tim simond

DIVE IN STYLE

SNORKEL | DIVE | UNWIND

SECOND EDITION

With 758 color illustrations

 Thames & Hudson

For my favourite budDee

First published in 2006 in hardcover in the United States of America
by Thames & Hudson Inc., 500 Fifth Avenue, New York, New York 10110

thamesandhudsonusa.com

This revised paperback edition 2010

Library of Congress Catalog Card Number 2009902121

ISBN 978-0-500-28630-2

Printed and bound in China by C&C Offset Printing Co. Ltd, China

contents

introduction 8

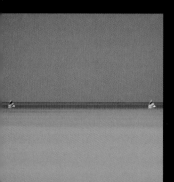

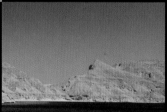

INTRODUCTION

'Staying on top of the water is like standing outside the circus tent.' With two-thirds of our planet covered in water, there's truth in this quip. Recreational diving is a new sport, really only available since the 1960s, and then only for the adventurous. Indeed, even 15 years ago, the image was of a small band of hardcore enthusiasts clad in unflattering neoprene, living in barrack-like accommodation and engaged in what was seen as an extreme and uncomfortable sport.

Welcome to the new and improved *Dive in Style*. Virtually every single entry for the resorts has been updated to reflect the intervening years. In the first edition I searched out 26 of the world's best dive sites married to stylish hotels and boats and this time, with the same strict criteria, I have added six new contenders that have come to my attention in the past few years.

Today diving has changed beyond recognition, with over 20 million enthusiasts worldwide and nearly a million newcomers each year. It has also moved upmarket. The initial concept, and indeed the first edition of this book, were driven by the observation that while the appeal of diving had spread to all levels of society, genuine information on the subject had not. If you wanted a luxury holiday with great diving, where you could dive in small groups or learn without being part of a huge class, but your family wanted other distractions, would it be easy to find the right place to go? Unfortunately not. There were 'Dive Hotels', but no obvious luxury or stylish hotels with diving – style and diving appeared mutually exclusive. It was equally as hard to find out about snorkelling.

However, no longer. After many months of research, not only have I updated all the original reports, but I've also come up with six new resorts to add to the existing quota, all of which fulfil these criteria.

Whether you dive, snorkel, or just want to chill, staying at any of these destinations will make a fantastic holiday.

The featured hotels are spread all over the world, all in temperate waters, and stretch from the Mediterranean to the Maldives. Obviously, you cannot compare the diving experience over such a diverse spread, but every one in its own way is the best that each area of the world has to offer and they all have their own unique appeal. Whittled down from a now ever-increasing list, the final choices were all based on merit only, and none of them paid to be included.

As always, a serious consideration was families. 'Dive Hotels' tend to cater just for divers. It may be that you are the only diver in the family, but while you enjoy yourself, what does the rest of your family do? None of these hotels is really a dedicated dive resort with the possible exception of Wakatobi, a new entrant; they are all just wonderful resorts in their own right, which cater for divers as much as they cater for tennis or any other sport, and this makes them very different. Consequently, I have looked at their restaurants, spas, excursions, facilities and especially snorkelling in order to provide a general view of the resort, not only a diver's perspective. This is not just a dive book; you could happily holiday at any of these resorts without even thinking of diving and still have an amazing time.

In the first edition I only used my own photographs to show these hotels in a realistic light, but this time I simply could not revisit all the resorts. Consequently, while the old rules apply to the new resorts, no models, no sets, no carefully arranged food or champagne picnics, with the original resorts in just a very few instances I have included one or two new images supplied by the resorts. The criteria for underwater images remains: every photograph was taken during our short stay, so if I saw something, there is a good chance that you will too – there has been no rush to a photo library for a shot of a rare mimic octopus, a creature that still eludes me. However, I did finally track down and attempt to photograph the impossibly tiny and amazing pygmy seahorse in Wakatobi, and while I did see the great hammerhead shark in Vamizi and the Turks and Caicos, there is no photograph in the book as in one instance it was too far away and in another too close. The rule is that if I did not see it, then it's not in the book and the overall aim remains simply to show what I saw, both on land and underwater.

In an effort to give you the most up-to-date information I have established a blog at www.diveinstyle.com on which any immediate updates or feedback will be posted.

UNDERWATER PHOTOGRAPHY

There is so much that goes into this hobby that I could do no better than refer you to experts. Ocean Optics of London (www.oceanoptics. co.uk) will give you totally unbiased advice, and while I am the first to look for a discount, this was one time I was happy to pay sticker price; they know their business and will give honest advice, even to the extent of losing themselves a sale.

GETTING THERE – DIVE IN STYLE AND ORIGINAL TRAVEL

Dive in Style features the best 26 hotels and boats in the 26 best dive spots in the world, but – by nature of their very remoteness – many of these are complicated to reach. As a result, I am delighted to confirm my continued partnership for this second edition with award-winning travel company Original Travel, who can make the diving dreams on these pages an effortless reality.

Original Travel is based in London and specializes in arranging tailor-made luxury holidays around the world. Their expert consultants know all the destinations in *Dive in Style* well, and can talk you through these memorable dive spots, taking care of every detail from flights to accommodation and activities.

Booking your dive holiday through Original Travel comes with additional benefits beyond competitive prices and expert advice, as every person who books will receive exciting and exclusive benefits at each of the *Dive in Style* destinations. Details of the latest offers will appear on the *Dive in Style* website alongside regularly updated news on the dive destinations.

For full details and prices for all the holidays in the book, as well as other *Dive in Style* destinations, check out www.diveinstyle.com or www.originaltravel.co.uk. Alternatively, you can call one of Original Travel's expert team on +44 (0)20 7978 7333.

Visible from space and stretching halfway up the eastern coast of Australia, the Great Barrier Reef is home to an incredible diversity of marine life. From the cooler waters in the south to the more temperate waters in the north, you'll find some 1,500 species of fish alone, as well as over 400 kinds of coral.

This colossus of a barrier reef has not been immune to the effects of El Niño and global warming, but somehow the north seems to have escaped – most notably around Ribbon Reef 10, a few miles from Lizard Island. Remote enough for you to escape the hordes of day trippers, Lizard Island gives you access to the kind of diving that is normally the exclusive preserve of live-aboards.

A three-hour flight from Sydney takes you to Cairns, the jumping-off spot for Lizard Island. While Cairns itself is nothing special, it's worth exploring the coast running north towards Cape Tribulation, which is unique for having more than 2,000,000 acres of rainforest running directly into the ocean.

While the Great Barrier Reef is protected as a World Heritage site, Lizard Island also enjoys the status of a marine park. It seems almost contradictory for such a pristine natural environment to be paired with a world-class hotel, yet that's exactly what makes this the perfect place to discover the world's largest reef system.

Gazing down from the plane, it's easy enough to see why these are called the Ribbon Reefs: the breaking surf forms a series of wavy white lines against the deep turquoise ocean. The individual reefs are identified not with names but numbers: Ribbon Reef 1 is next door to Ribbon Reef 2, and so on. This no-nonsense approach is typically Australian: it's simple but it works.

lizard island

HOTEL

LIZARD ISLAND

lizard island lodge

Located close to Ribbon Reef 10, Lizard Island hosts the northernmost island resort on the Great Barrier Reef, as well as a marine research station and a large number of the monitor lizards from which it takes its name. Despite being so close to the tropics, this 2,500-acre pocket of land is somewhat barren due to the constant wind and lack of rainfall, but don't let that put you off: its shores are lined with 24 white-sand beaches, which alone are worth the trip. Lizard Island Lodge occupies the most beautiful and protected of these. Originally built in 1975 and now part of the exclusive Voyages group, this exclusive retreat combines the very best in accommodation with access to some truly spectacular diving.

A three-minute ride from the island's simple airstrip delivers you to the hotel's discreet single-storey lodge, a wide, wooden-floored expanse with deep wicker sofas and timber chairs that sets the tone of laid-back luxury. Radiating out like wings on either side of the lodge are the rooms, usually arranged in pairs, which feature bright, modern Australian-style decor. All open directly onto shady private terraces; some offer a daybed, while others provide a hammock. Your experience will depend on where you stay. The Sunset Villas, built on the gently sloping hillside above Sunset Beach, are set in natural bush, while the Anchor Bay Suites and Rooms, each

at a glance

Airport	Cairns via Sydney
Airlines	Qantas or British Airways, then Macair to Lizard Island (baggage weight limit 20kg)
Transfer time	55 mins by plane
Rooms	40 (all air-conditioned)
Staff ratio	1+
Activities	Walks, glass-bottom boat tours, research station visits, fishing, catamarans, dinghies, beach picnics, Elemis spa, gym, swimming pool, tennis, glass-bottom paddle skis, snorkel lessons
Services	Internet, television, Bose sound system, DVD in Guest Departure Lounge
Children	12+
Power type	3-pin angled flat
Currency	Australian dollar
GMT	+10
Booking	www.diveinstyle.com

with their own white-sand track leading to the main beach, are fronted by a rolling green lawn, palms, pine trees and sea roses. The former give a sense of being in the Australian bush; the latter have the feel of a beach holiday. For the best of both worlds, the lofty Pavilion or 'Pavy' delivers, and comes complete with your own private pool.

The resort's impact on the island's environment is minimal; nature has been tamed, but there are no manicured flowerbeds. Instead, you'll come across some much more interesting features, such as the seemingly permanently occupied sunbird's nest that hangs adjacent to the bar, or the monitor lizards drinking from your giant clam footbath…it's here that the resort just morphs into nature.

As expected, the food represents the best of Australian fusion cooking. With the exception of private beachside picnics, meals are served in the lodge's semi-circular dining pavilion overlooking the beach and the ocean beyond. There are no

windows or walls to separate you from the great outdoors – this is alfresco, Aussie-style.

While you're here, you can do as much or as little as you like. At your disposal is a fleet of fully prepared motorized dinghies that will take you, along with a serious picnic hamper, to any beach you desire. You can also walk to remote bays, trek up to Cook's Point for the view or take a glass-bottom boat tour. If you prefer to stay put, there are plenty of options for relaxing. The freshwater swimming pool is great for chilling out, or you can spoil yourself with treatments based on marine ingredients at the Azure Spa.

When it's time to go, there's the Guest Departure Lounge, which lets you enjoy yourself up until the last minute. Room check-out is in the late morning, but most flights leave in the afternoon; here you can take advantage of showers, bathrooms and suitcase storage. It's a final touch of hospitality that makes for a sweet end to your stay at Lizard Island – a very special bolthole with an Antipodean flavour, where 'no worries' means just that.

Located opposite the fleet of bobbing yellow dinghies at the western end of the hotel's beach, the Beach Club features a classroom, storage rooms, hanging racks and even a small dive shop. A full range of top-class gear is available, but if you bring your own, one of the friendly team will collect it from your room and look after it throughout your stay.

DIVE CENTER

The boat for Barrier Reef excursions is the comfortable, beamy 53-ft MV Serranidae, which provides plenty of dry cover and an upper sun deck; for trips closer to home, the 42-ft Monitor is used and if you want a private charter then 51 ft of Riviera can be yours. Every other day there are full-day excursions to outer reef dive sites, including the world-famous Cod Hole. On other days half-day excursions to closer reef systems are offered. When booking, just check that your dates don't coincide with the very rare bad tides or else you might not be able to dive. You can now pre-book online, which I would strongly recommend.

On arrival at the dive sites, an army of staff swing into a ballet of action to moor the boat between the stunning shallow reefs. Access is by a giant stride off a sea-level platform, and returning to the boat couldn't be easier: your gear is lifted off your back and the bottle changed, leaving you free to enjoy the full-on buffet lunch. For divers or snorkellers, this trip is a must.

It's a shame that no courses are offered at such a flawless dive operation, but it's still possible to do your open-water certification dives. Let them know in advance if you are doing your pool work elsewhere so they can tell you what documents to bring; their rules are strict, but safety is at the forefront of their minds.

at a glance

Boats	53 ft (dry, covered), 42 ft (covered)
Group size	6
Instructors	8+
Languages	English
Courses	Resort and refresher courses; open-water qualification dives, subject to conditions
Children	14+
Other	Computer hire, superb food and drinks, gear prep and wash down, private charters, dive shop

Exploring the Great Barrier Reef is a truly memorable experience, especially in these still relatively untouched northern waters. The size, variety and sheer quantity of corals and sea life have to be seen to be believed, and you never know what you might encounter on each dive – there always seems to be something different. For non-divers, the snorkelling is utterly superb; you can float over the reefs' truly pristine sun-dappled shallows and not miss a thing.

DIVING

Cod Hole is the best-known dive site, renowned for its friendly or perhaps simply greedy giant potato cod. The dive begins with controlled feeding at roughly 30 ft: you kneel on the sea floor while 80lb-plus cod swim around you, waiting for lunch to be shared out by your guide. In exchange for the meal, they happily put up with being gently stroked. For snorkellers, they lure the cod up to you.

While this is fun, it's worth splitting off as soon as you can to explore the outer reef wall, which drops down to roughly 70 ft before reaching the main drop-off. An easy dive, it is home to clownfish, Napoleon wrasse, bumphead parrotfish, green moray, lionfish...the list goes on. But what really sets this site apart is the condition and sheer quantity of the brilliant multi-coloured corals, including truly wonderful blue and turquoise staghorns.

New Reef is a gentle, shallow dive, with acres of perfect staghorn and cabbage corals. Its aquarium-like beauty is just as good for snorkelling: you can spend hours in a few feet of water, picking over the coral and spotting anything from tiny flatworms to what must be some of the world's most enormous clams, at around 4 ft long. There's also Dynamite Pass, which can be either an easy dive or, if the current is flowing, a drift dive. Along with all the usual

at a glance

Local sites	2, plus endless sites on Great Barrier Reef (weather dependent)
Level	Easy
Visibility	100 ft on outer reef; 50 ft on inner reef
Must-dives	Cod Hole, Dynamite Pass, No Name Reef
Snorkelling	Excellent on house reef, superb from dive boat
Wetsuits	5mm (3mm in summer)
Coral	Pristine
Marine life	Giant clams, giant potato cod, Napoleon wrasse, bumphead parrotfish, humpback and minke whale, manta ray, shark, green moray, lionfish, clownfish
Other	Hyperbaric chamber at Townsville (2 hrs), day trips to barrier reef and inner reef on alternate days, marine park

TOP LEFT
You can snorkel among dozens of giant clams, some over a hundred years old, at Mrs Watson's Clam Garden. A marine biologist will be your guide.

OPPOSITE, ABOVE AND BELOW
The sheer quantity, quality and variety of coral on the Great Barrier Reef is simply breathtaking.

suspects, you are almost guaranteed to come across an inquisitive (and hungry) Napoleon wrasse, as well as sleeping white-tip reef sharks. With reasonable air consumption, you can expect to spend well over an hour underwater on all these dives, so at least a 5 mm wetsuit is a must.

Closer to home, North Direction Island (so called thanks to the straightforward Aussie naming system) and Magillivrays Reef tend to offer less visibility but wonderful diving. The fringe reef surrounding the former is sheltered from prevailing winds so conditions are never really a problem. Ranging from about 15 ft to 40 ft in depth, the fine sandy floor is dotted with coral bommies, and you drift gently from one to another marvelling at the sea life, all of which are simply a cornershop version of the main event.

Returning from the day trip, a final treat awaits you: fish feeding, with a difference. Two 9-ft-long nurse sharks come to the dive platform, behaving like a pair of puppies fighting for attention. You may also notice a dark brown shadow lurking in the water; this is Simon, a 500lb-plus, 8-ft-long giant Queensland grouper. He'll surface when the smell of fish proves too much for him, but he's blisteringly fast, so don't even think of looking away.

LEFT
Snorkelling with green turtles off Casurina Beach, a great place for a picnic.

RIGHT
The Great Barrier Reef is where the real Nemo lives.

BELOW
An octopus looks unfazed as it poses for the camera.

OPPOSITE
Giant potato cod are so large that they don't feel threatened by divers.

BELOW
A pair of large nurse shark regularly visit the dive platform, greedy for food and attention.

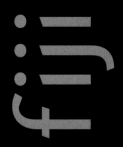

There was a time when the Fijians would rather eat you than greet you, but today the dreaded 'Cannibal Isles' are home to quite possibly the friendliest people on the planet. The country's blend of cultures is fascinating, and although there has been some well-publicized trouble between the indigenous Fijians and the Fijian Indians, this ethnic divide generally simmers in the background and should not be a deterrent to visiting.

Consisting of over 330 islands, Fiji has a population of only 850,000, 75 per cent of whom live on the main island of Viti Levu. This leaves at least 329 islands for the remaining few; many islands are deserted. Thus the pace of life drops once you make it to the outer islands, and 'crowd' becomes just another word in the dictionary.

Viti Levu is primarily given over to more mass-market hotels; you will almost certainly need to stay in one at some point due to airline schedules. The best option for overnighting is the Sheraton Royal Denarau, about a 20-minute drive from the airport. While the mainland has its attractions, it's best not to spend too much time here: you will only discover the true beauty of this stunning archipelago by venturing further afield.

While all the outlying Fijian islands are truly beautiful, to experience the very best diving the country has to offer a 45-minute luxury flight almost due north will deposit you on Wakaya, your dream private island.

The chances are that you might spend less than an hour on Fiji before undergoing a seamless transition to the island's private and luxurious turboprop for the short flight north. Passing over the startling verdant hills of Viti Levu, and then the turquoise waters and glittering reefs, after a 40-minute flight the private island of Wakaya comes into view.

wakaya

HOTEL wakaya club

'Bula', or welcome, to your 2,200-acre island home, less than ten per cent of which has been terraformed into one man's dream, the balance left to nature, stuffed with wild deer, horses, goats and pigs. Ten minutes in a 4 x 4 and the resort reveals itself, small and intimate, no soaring reception, just ten discreet rooms set in beautiful and lush tropical gardens all fronting onto the multi-hued Koro Sea.

Initially there is little that obviously impresses, which might come as a disappointment, but that is indeed the discreet charm of Wakaya, how so very low key and intimate it is. This probably explains its allure to many of Hollywood's A list over the past 20 years, including Keith Richards, who notoriously fell out of a tree and probably gave this off-the-radar resort more publicity than it has ever sought. The contrast with the world you have left is marked and you immediately feel a world apart.

It would be a stretch to describe this resort as truly stylish; it is, however, a beautiful, incredibly well-maintained traditional resort interwoven with local Fijian culture that could well have been opened yesterday, so fastidious is its upkeep. Crafted out of a coconut plantation and built within the towering palms are a smattering of buildings, while behind are an immaculate nine-hole golf course, tennis courts, croquet lawn, gym and just about any other facility you could require.

at a glance

Airport	Nadi
Airlines	Air New Zealand, Air Pacific, Korean Air
Transfer time	40 mins flight by turboprop, 10 mins by 4 x 4
Rooms	10 (all air-conditioned)
Staff ratio	10+
Activities	Tennis, croquet, boules, nine-hole golf, spa, fly and deep-sea fishing, hiking, nature walks, gym, billiards, kava ceremony, spa
Services	Room service
Children	16+
Power type	3-pin angled flat
Currency	Fijian dollar, US dollar
GMT	+10
Booking	www.diveinstyle.com

Regardless of what time of day you arrive, this is the only resort in the world I know of where your room *will* be ready and late check-out a given: they simply do not book your room the day before or the day after your reservation. The rooms are spacious with separate bedroom and sitting room, all in traditional Fijian style with a high-eaved roof, woven walls and timber floors, and while not particularly exciting in comparison to more contemporary resorts, have every facility you could want. The luxurious and more stylish bathrooms offer a full bath and striking glass-walled external shower. For two couples travelling together, the Governor's Bure is a relative bargain with two even more generous bedroom suites and a shared sitting room.

The main beach, once a wide band of striking ground white coral sand, has lost much of its splendour due to recent cyclones, although it is now once again starting to accrete. However, since it is a private island you are not limited to one beach, with private picnics on deserted beaches being an option. A mass of activities are available including a spa, or you can just wallow in the incredible peace and tranquility of the island.

Lunch and dinner are announced by the beating of the Fijian drum made of a hollowed-out trunk, its dull 'thunk' calling the lazy guests out of their reverie; breakfast, thoughtfully, is left to you. Led by the island CEO, himself a former chef, his presence is still felt every day, despite the fact that the head chef has been with him for 19 years. As a consequence, between them, every meal is a treat – just a few simple choices that will suit any palate. It is all utterly delicious and there is always a choice of local fresh fish cooked to perfection and, weather permitting, every meal is served on the wide shady terrace overlooking the beach, the space between diners providing total privacy.

The owner has done much for this island and there can be no better testament to his efforts than the fact that all the staff, if they are old enough, have been here since its inception. The staff are always delighted to see you, and genuinely so. Yes, the price may shock, but included in the tariff is some of the best food you can imagine, limitless champagne if that is your thing, utter solitude and two dives a day for each of you.

To call this a dive resort is ridiculous, but since the price does include diving, it could be considered as such. It is therefore easy to pronounce this as easily the best dive resort in the world and, as for the diving, also some of the very best. I need to return.

If you aren't good on boats, Wakaya has to offer the easiest, most comfortable, convenient top-class diving in Fiji, and very probably the world. Come to think of it, I cannot think of anywhere where such incredible diving is so immediately accessible – nearly all the sites are less than five minutes from the dock, which is just 30 seconds from the dive shop.

DIVE CENTER

If you meet after a leisurely and truly exceptional breakfast at 9.30 a.m., you can have done two dives and return well in time for lunch, leaving the rest of the day to explore the island or just chill; or if you want, dive some more. The only delay that might occur is the sight of pilot whales basking on the surface, which I witnessed, a wonderful sight.

The center, occupying an enviable position at the end of the beach, is small, perfectly formed and equipped with a good range of mostly Scubapro gear, but my standard mantra about bring your own mask applies even here. All the dive sites are so close that the boats are more than up to the job. If there are just two of you, then the chances are you will use the 20-ft aluminium monohull for the five-minute trip, or if you are off to one of the more distant sites (relative, in that Saxophone, the most distant, is only 15 minutes away) or if there are more of you, the *Flying Wakaya*, a 26-ft catamaran, is the usual method of transport. Dives are normally around 10 a.m., or any time you want them, and while two dives a day are included in the tariff, if you are up for more then Meli and his team are always keen, never seeming to tire of the diving here. While it really is fantastic, I cannot help but fantasize that given all the available reefs in the area there must surely be even more amazing sites just waiting to be discovered. However, what is available is so good and so close to shore that you can understand why there is no rush.

at a glance

Boats	20 and 26 ft
Group size	4+
Instructors	1
Languages	English
Courses	All PADI
Children	12+
Other	Gear prep and wash down, computer hire

ABOVE
The reefs veritably bristle with darting anthias of every hue.

Possibly aside from the Sonosoma Strait, this has to be the best diving in Fiji. It is certainly the easiest, most convenient, most uncrowded and most comfortable diving in Fiji, and it is just minutes from the dock. Don't plan on kicking back and enjoying the ride, you will just have time to don your wetsuit and clean your mask before it's time to get wet.

DIVING

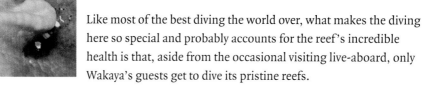

Like most of the best diving the world over, what makes the diving here so special and probably accounts for the reef's incredible health is that, aside from the occasional visiting live-aboard, only Wakaya's guests get to dive its pristine reefs.

Setting this reef system apart from so many is not only the startling overall health, but also the combination of both healthy hard and soft corals – bleaching is something only for clothes. Yes, Fiji is renowned for its soft corals and is known as the soft coral capital of the world, but here the hard corals are an even more spectacular addition. Truly gargantuan brain corals, layers of plate corals that disappear into the depths, star corals, finger corals, and the most spectacular of all, a bright red brain coral, bright red without the need for flash, something I have never seen anywhere else – truly extraordinary.

When you have finished marvelling at this rare site of pristine corals often cloaked in clouds of blue, orange and purple anthias, the giant fans, the brilliant soft corals, then there is the marine life proper. From manta to ghost pipefish, hammerhead to blue ribbon eel, leaf scorpionfish to nudibranchs, they are all here and Meli and his local team know where they live. But in the unlikely event that you see none of these, the clouds of anthias and spectacular corals are enough in themselves.

at a glance

Local sites	15
Level	Easy to intermediate
Visibility	100 ft
Must-dives	Lion's Den, Saxophone, Hell's Gate, Homestead Passage
Snorkelling	Very good snorkelling trips and good house reef accessed from the beach
Wetsuits	3mm max all year
Coral	Superb hard and soft
Marine life	Leaf scorpionfish, white-tip shark, hammerhead shark, manta ray, grey reef shark, blue ribbon eels, pilot whales, Maori wrasse
Other	Night dives, hyperbaric chamber in Suva

ABOVE
Big schools of jack always seem to turn up on the point at Saxophone, one of the many great dives.

ABOVE
Endless hues of perfect soft
corals, seen here closed up.

RIGHT
The reefs are among the
healthiest in Fiji and some
of the best in the world.
Hard and soft corals full
to bursting with life.

ABOVE
Perfect and pristine hard
corals are everywhere; here
bleaching is just for washing.

BELOW
Not for nothing is Fiji known
as the soft coral capital of the
world. A veritable flower stall.

OPPOSITE, ABOVE, LEFT
Giant fans are everywhere, this
time blasted with purple anthias.

OPPOSITE, ABOVE, RIGHT
The home of leaf scorpionfish
of every colour is known to Meli
and his team.

OPPOSITE, BELOW, LEFT
Stop, relax and study the reefs
and you will find all sorts of life.

OPPOSITE, BELOW, RIGHT
Manta ray are pretty much on
demand.

RIGHT
The cave at Saxophone with its
dramatic exit into the blue.

BELOW, RIGHT
The most remarkable large
tomato brain coral which,
incredibly, is this colour
without artificial light! I have
never seen this anywhere else.

While the weather should always enable you to dive Homestead
and Lion's Den, two of the must-dives, if it is good, demand
Saxophone. It starts as a wide, non-claustrophobic sink hole
that drops down in the reef until opening up to the face at
about 70 ft. Passing through this cavern you then drift down
to the fields of coral, the deepest part being an unusual point
sticking out into the current where it is worth just hanging,
watching the passing life: turtle, schools of jack and manta ray.
Then pick your way back over the incredible fields of sloping
pristine coral filled with life. You could spend hours on this
dive alone.

Simply put, I did not stay long enough and to this day I regret
all the dive sites I missed. I should have dived in the afternoon
as well as in the morning and also added a few night dives for
good measure, but such is the relaxed pace of Wakaya that this
thought only came to me somewhat late in the day; don't make
the same mistake. So, if you can find the budget for a five-day
stay, I urge you to dive morning, noon and night and given the
need for 24 hours to bleed off the nitrogen before flying, plan
to leave on a Sunday or a Monday and this way you won't waste
a day of diving; given that Fiji is a truly Christian society, Sunday
is an enforced day of rest.

Crystalline turquoise waters, pure white sand, swaying palms, cobalt blue sky... add to all this the colourful and exotic culture of the Polynesians, plus a twist of French (most especially in the kitchen), and you have something truly special. Tahiti, Bora Bora, Moorea, Huahine, Manihi, Rangiroa, Fakarava – just the evocative names of these islands are enough to get you through the travel agent's door.

There is, however, one drawback: you won't find Papeete listed alongside Tokyo and London as one of the world's most expensive cities – but it should be. That aside, once you have made the pilgrimage to this remote part of the world, it is well worth taking in three or even four islands. Flight schedules mean you normally have to spend a night in Papeete at the beginning and end of your trip. But unless you're a Gauguin fanatic or plan to explore the beautiful interior, you will probably want to give Tahiti herself a miss as – surprisingly – this is not really a beach destination since there is no natural white sand here.

Spread over an area nine times the size of their mother country, the islands that make up French Polynesia are composed primarily, although not exclusively, of the Society Islands and the Tuamotus. Linked by Air Tahiti Nui's domestic arm, the former are extraordinarily beautiful volcanic islands with lofty peaks clad in verdant jungle; the latter, low-lying coral atolls strung out like pearls (and also producing them). These island groups are separated by only a few hundred miles, but it might as well be a few thousand, so different is the experience.

Hotel Bora Bora has finally caved in to her need for some major surgery and has closed until at least 2011. So, in a fortuitous and timely manner, the Four Seasons Bora Bora has picked up the banner as the island's top resort and opened about the most inclusive and extensive resort you could imagine, and in a magical position. But like everything in these islands, it all comes at a price.

HOTEL

four seasons bora bora

Your arrival, after a brief 45-minute flight from Papeete, is as good as it gets anywhere in the world. This simply has to be the airport of choice, relaxed, unhurried and perched on the water's edge with no cars in sight. The resort is also set out on the motu, a string of white-beached islets wrapped around the gradually subsiding Mount Otemanu, and separated from it by clear turquoise-hued waters. There are no roads to this airport, you and your bags are shepherded by welcoming Four Seasons staff and ushered to immaculate, distinctive blue-hulled FS boats that tie up mere feet from the arrivals hall and ten minutes later deposit you, Venice like, at the hotel reception. Indeed, here you are even closer to the water. Unarguably *the* way to arrive at a hotel.

This is no boutique resort with over a hundred rooms, but it does have space, and lots of it. Almost all the rooms are hovering on stilts over the translucent lagoon and are reached via long wooden tails spearing out from the fringing beach, while the few villas are on the motu itself with their own private beaches. The balance of the fast-maturing 55 acres is devoted purely to the resort's endless facilities and as a result it has dedicated areas for just about every age group. Nature created it as three separate motus or islets, but now it is effectively one, joined through a series of bridges over meandering calm lagoons and inlets, home to

at a glance

Airport	Bora Bora via Papeete
Airlines	Air New Zealand, Air Tahiti Nui, Air France, Qantas, Hawaiian Airlines, Lan Chile
Transfer time	10 mins by boat
Rooms	100 and 7 villas (all air-conditioned), some with private pool
Staff ratio	2+
Activities	Spa, fitness, yoga, tennis, badminton, snorkelling, pool, endless watersports, kids activities for all seasons, teen center, kite surfing, parasailing, fishing, chapel, waverunners, kayaking, gym, spa
Services	Wi-fi, telephone, 2 plasmas, DVD, CD, satellite television, room service, mobile phones
Children	Any age, babysitters available
Power type	2-pin round
Currency	French Pacific franc
GMT	-10
Booking	www.diveinstyle.com

juvenile eagle rays and ideal for gentle snorkelling. More importantly, this is one of the only locations I know where you can actually look back from your bungalow over transparent turquoise waters at the haunting outline of your island home; traditionally you look out to sea. The staggering profile of the island of Bora Bora is surely one of the great sites of the world and justly claims its title of 'world's most beautiful island'. To wake up each and every morning to this beautiful and dominant presence is fortunate in the extreme, and if you are lucky enough to have room 330, then you really are in the front row.

Although only recently opened, the extensive gardens are already lush, a scented walkway at night with hints of frangipani, gardenia and tiare, the latter so evocative that Chef Gilles has even created an ice cream using its essence. And that is not all he has created as dinner at Ari Moana will validate, especially for seafood lovers. The food is superb, breakfast poolside at Ari Moana, lunch at Fare Hoa Beach Bar, dinner on the terrace at Tere Nui and sushi at the Sunset Bar. Interspersed with the occasional themed Italian dinner, you are unlikely to get bored.

Aside from the villas, all the rooms are overwater bungalows or suites, set on stilts far out into the lagoon with ladders down to clear, safe swimming. What you see, however, depends on what you pay. If you want the magical view of Mount Otemanu, then you will have to pay more than if you settle for a lagoon view. And should you wish to up the ante there are six larger suites with small plunge pools set at the furthest reaches of the walkways. The wooden bungalows are all beautifully fitted out with every modern convenience and have separate bedrooms and sitting rooms, unusually but effectively separated by the generous bathroom. Each room has vast sliding windows onto your terrace with direct access to the ocean, but the best part is the ability to lie in the huge double bath with the sliding doors rolled back and just gaze at the view. Best bathroom view ever?

This resort is aimed unashamedly at the family market but in a way to ensure that there is also space and peace for adults. Aside from endless watersports, including waverunners ideal for a DIY round-island tour, there is a world-class spa and just about anything else you could wish for. Given the endless facilities and activities set aside for children and teenagers you will be lucky to see them again. In short, an awesome family holiday, or as Robert Louis Stevenson remarked on his arrival in these islands in 1888, 'I threw one look to either hand, and knew I was in Fairyland'.

Since I last visited the islands, a new force had emerged in dive operators, Bathys Diving. Someone has finally decided to invest serious money and create the number one dive operator both in Moorea and Bora Bora; they have succeeded. Simply put, it's probably the best equipped dive operation you are liable to find anywhere.

DIVE CENTER

New immaculate custom-built dive boats, new SeaQuest BCs and Aqualung regs, embossed towels, fresh fruit between dives, camera table, fridge and safety equipment; an experienced diver has really thought out this design. It's all very well having the gear, but it is also run by the nicest bunch of French and Polynesians you could hope for and nitrox is available at no additional charge as is the timely pick-up from your hotel. If you feel like splashing out, then a private dive to Tapu is well worth the extra cost, provided you take the opportunity to be the first boat there for your appointment with the lemon shark.

Find your way to the Four Seasons' jetty at 8.15 a.m. and you are probably only 15 minutes away from the outer reef and the principal base where you may be transferred to another boat, depending on the group size. However, little time is lost as the base is opposite the main pass so you would need to drop by anyway. A further five or ten minutes takes you to the best diving.

Unusually, but aided by free nitrox and shallow second dives, there is only a short 40-minute surface interval when fresh fruit and chilled water are served, ensuring that you are back at the Four Seasons in time for lunch and the thorny question of how to spend the afternoon. Top notch.

at a glance

Boats	24 ft (wet, covered)
Group size	5
Instructors	7
Languages	English, French
Courses	All PADI
Children	8+
Other	Drinks, gear prep and wash down, private charters, aqua safari (helmet diving, no tanks, no experience necessary)
Website	www.bathys-diving.com

It is still all about pelagics, principally shark, and if you have an innate fear of them then this is the perfect opportunity for 'in at the deep end' therapy. This is the only place in the world I know where, albeit thanks to the questionable act of feeding, you are guaranteed close encounters with burly and reclusive three-metre lemon shark, along with droves of the more common grey reef and black-tip reef shark.

DIVING

On arrival at Tapu do not be surprised to see your instructor breaking all the rules and taking a giant stride into shark-infested waters with fish heads stuffed into his BC and inviting you to follow. While initially somewhat alarming, this practice has been ongoing for years incident free. It can, however, become somewhat of an underwater circus depending on group size and the smaller the group, the more enthralling the experience as your guide taunts the circling shark; this is one dive where it is worth taking a private charter if you really want to be guaranteed close-up action.

Yes, feeding is questionable, however, there is no other way you will regularly encounter fat lemon shark at such close quarters almost on demand. A word of advice: unlike many other shark, lemon swim inches above the reef so if you want to max the thrill you need to get down as low as you can so as to meet them face to face, otherwise you will just see their grey backs. While normally I would counsel about not touching the coral while seeking handholds, since the Crown of Thorns starfish has eaten most of it, this is not really an issue. This is unquestionably the best all-round dive, starting with lemon shark and then working your way up the water column seeing white-mouthed morays, green morays,

at a glance

Local sites	10+
Level	Easy to advanced
Visibility	100 ft outside reef; 40 ft inside reef
Must-dives	Muri Muri, Tapu, Tupitipiti
Snorkelling	Superb on house reef, very good from dive boat
Wetsuits	3mm
Coral	Excellent
Marine life	Grey reef shark, lemon shark, black-tip reef shark, manta ray, eagle ray, schools of barracuda, humpback whale, tuna, Napoleon wrasse, dolphin
Other	Hyperbaric chamber on Tahiti (1 hr), night dives

OPPOSITE, CLOCKWISE FROM TOP LEFT
Triggerfish are the only predator of the Crown of Thorns that have gorged on the reefs. Regretfully the beautiful triton shell, their natural predator, is more commonly found for sale than on reefs; walls of clams of limitless colours decorate the channels; even though the coral is virtually dead, there is no shortage of life; Crown of Thorns may be the scourge of the reefs, but is fascinating in detail.

octopus, giant triggerfish, turtle, schools of barracuda and
always accompanied by a veritable flotilla of vibrant tropical
fish, hoping that the stench on your instructor's wetsuit suggests
there may be something left over for them. And just when you
least expect it, the circling lemon shark return in case they
were right.

At Muri Muri grey and black-tip reef shark, a dozen or more,
show no fear and will approach closely circling throughout the
dive. Once the feeding is over, enjoy the vast schools of jacks or
the incredibly approachable turtle who seem to seek you out and
are happy to swim right at you: I couldn't even get my camera to
focus as they attempted to feed on the lens.

If you search for manta then with the sad absence of the Hotel
Bora Bora dock, the site at Anau will probably deliver squadrons
of eagle rays and endless anemones with their attendant
clownfish, albeit that visibility is always fairly poor in the
channel itself. Encounters with these gentle giants are always
thrilling and here at the beginning and end of the dive you will
find spectacular coral, seemingly protected from the Crown of
Thorns by the barrier reef.

While the diving is unrivalled for shark action, it can become
somewhat repetitive. Consequently either you need a private
charter to take you further afield, or if you are here just for the
diving then a week is long enough, leaving you scope to visit
Tiki-Hau or even the fantastic Rangiroa, once Kia Ora reopens
from its somewhat overdue refurbishment.

The main islet of Tikehau isn't much to look at – it's a remote coral atoll whose flat surface never rises more than a few inches above sea level. But don't be fooled by appearances: it's worth coming here for the diving alone. What's more, just a 15-minute boat ride away is the small private motu that is home to the luxurious Pearl Beach Resort.

tikehau

HOTEL

pearl beach tikehau

Established in 1990, this oasis of a resort was substantially remodelled and expanded in 2001. Built in the traditional Polynesian style, with palm-thatched roofs and woven bamboo walls, it now boasts 37 rooms. Virtually all have air-conditioning, but the island's constant wind and efficient ceiling fans mean you probably won't need it. Leave doors and windows open and you will be lulled to sleep by the sound of lapping water, as that is all there is to hear.

You can choose to stay on the beach or over the water. The beach bungalows are set amid waving palms on a thin strip of pinkish sand, which is not exactly powdery but does offer good shallow swimming and snorkelling; these rooms are all the same size and feature raised decks and internal–external bathrooms. The overwater rooms come as standard bungalows, most of which enjoy views over the lagoon, and premium bungalows, which have direct access to the lagoon.

For the best and biggest rooms, make a beeline for the newest overwater suites. These are reached via a 300-ft timber walkway stretching over the transparent lagoon, and are even more tranquil; for the ultimate in seclusion, opt for room 45 at the very end of the resort. These overwater suites host a generous sitting area, wooden floors and French doors that give onto your own private deck. This is spacious enough to

at a glance

Airport	Tikehau via Papeete
Airlines	Air New Zealand, Air Tahiti Nui, Qantas, Air France
Transfer time	15 mins by boat
Rooms	37 (most air-conditioned)
Staff ratio	3+
Activities	Bird island trip, village trip, desert island picnics, kayaking, swimming pool, volleyball, *pétanque*, spa, ping pong, billiards, jet ski
Services	Telephone, television, CD player, room service, safe
Children	12+
Power type	2-pin round
Currency	French Pacific franc, US dollar
GMT	-10
Telephone	+689 962300
Booking	www.diveinstyle.com

accommodate two comfy wooden loungers along with a covered eating area, and provides total privacy. A lower-level swimming platform has a shower and steps leading into the water – snorkelling couldn't be easier. Wake up early and you might catch some small (harmless) black-tip reef sharks or eagle rays in the sands and coral heads beneath you.

People staying in the beach bungalows are often puzzled as to why, after an excellent dinner, fellow guests can be seen shamelessly ferrying French bread back to their rooms. The mystery is solved by a look inside the overwater rooms: the design incorporates a glass floor panel that not only gives a view of the lagoon below, but also lets you drop bread through a hatchway. A novel way of creating a feeding frenzy, but in fact you're better off throwing bread from the deck – you'll create just as much mayhem and get a better view of the fish.

It's not just the fish that are well fed here; the guests are too. One of the great things about this part of the world is the French influence, especially when it comes to food. Breakfast includes fresh croissants, baguettes and *pains au chocolat*, while other meals, served at the

Porteho restaurant, are all based around a simple but delicious French-inspired menu that usually focuses on fresh local fish. The choice makes perfect sense in light of the cost of importing goods here; most things, including meat, are well travelled, coming from as far away as Australia or New Zealand. But so pampered are you at Pearl Beach that it's easy to forget the logistics behind the luxury.

Speaking of luxury in this remote outpost, since I last reported, the hotel has turned one room into an intimate Zen-like spa which offers a range of wonderful local treatments; a crucial addition to this hideaway.

All over the resort, the atmosphere is low-key and relaxed, with no apparent dress code. If you want to use the resort as a chill zone, you can lie on the sand or in the small freshwater infinity pool by the beach, and gaze out over the gin-clear waters of the sea; if you'd rather venture elsewhere, there is a limited range of activities available, from line fishing to lunch on a deserted motu. Whatever your priorities, Pearl Beach offers a true escape.

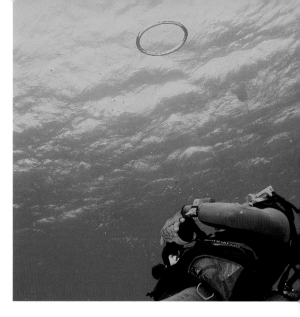

Squeezed next door to the front desk of Pearl Beach Tikehau, the dive center is small but perfectly placed. Run by English-speaking French instructors, it's a laid-back affair, and you're given the shortest indemnity form you're ever likely to sign. The briefing is simple: the main point is that by law the maximum diving depth is 100 ft unless you are suitably qualified.

DIVE CENTER

Dives are generally in the morning to take advantage of the sunlight, and a two-tank trip departs daily. You can choose from a good selection of Sherwood equipment; it is up to you to rig and then rinse it at the end of the day. The staff will stow and prepare it for your next excursion, but that is about the limit of it.

The boat is no-frills but adequate, and can take up to 12 divers. Space is somewhat limited and there is no real allowance for underwater cameras, although there is a small dry compartment. The dive sites are only a 25-minute ride across the lagoon, but be prepared to get wet if the sea gets choppy; you would be best advised to don your wetsuit before boarding.

Entry is by backward roll, but if you wish, the captain will help you put on and remove your gear in the water. Groups are of no more than five, a fact that enhances your sense of pathfinding, and dives are normally limited to about 50 minutes. Tea, water and biscuits are served during the surface intervals.

In short, this is a fairly basic dive operation that gets the job done. The most important thing is to remember where you are: you won't see another dive boat, so the sites are truly yours.

at a glance

Boats	24 ft (wet, covered)
Group size	5
Instructors	2
Languages	English, French
Courses	Qualification dives and advanced courses; no beginners' courses
Children	12+
Other	Drinks, gear prep
Website	www.bluenui.com

ABOVE
Acres of stunning virgin coral
greet you every time you dive
Tikehau's translucent waters.

The dive operation may be simple, but this hardly matters once you are underwater. The atoll of Tikehau was once described by Jacques Cousteau as richer in fish life than any other lagoon in the world. Although decades have gone by since then, it is still clearly exceptional.

DIVING

Like Rangiroa, its larger and more crowded neighbour, Tikehau has only one pass into the ocean, Tuheiva, and five out of the six dive sites are clustered around it. Luckily Pearl Beach is the only hotel in the area, so there is no competition for the moorings.

Without a doubt, Shark Hole takes the prize, and like all the sites, it has fantastic 100 ft-plus visibility. As you start your descent, you're guaranteed to see dozens of grey reef sharks circling beneath you; they will generally approach within 6 ft, and nearer if you're not looking. You're also bound to spot a friendly Napoleon wrasse gliding back and forth; it will also come quite close, though never quite close enough to show off its brilliant colouring. Turn to the wall itself and you'll see that it's literally alive, undulating with thousands upon thousands of squirrelfish.

Once you've made your way past these and the occasional hawksbill turtle, you end up in a spectacular coral garden. French Polynesia has no soft corals but it has good claim to be the world's hard coral capital, especially here on Tikehau with its seemingly endless fields stretching out before you. These shallow waters offer a truly fabulous sight: the sea is rarely deeper than 30 ft, and it is magical being underwater in such a pristine environment.

at a glance

Local sites	6
Level	Easy
Visibility	100 ft+
Must-dives	Shark Hole
Snorkelling	Very good from dive boat
Wetsuits	3mm
Coral	Pristine
Marine life	Grey reef shark, black-tip reef shark, hammerhead shark, white-tip reef shark, Napoleon wrasse, dolphin, schools of jackfish, schools of African pompanos, eagle ray
Other	Hyperbaric chamber on Tahiti (1 hr)

OPPOSITE, TOP
Tikehau's perfect corals
provide shelter for predators
and prey alike.

OPPOSITE, MAIN PICTURE
A diver soars over the abyss-
like drop-off with the brilliant
colours of a basket star in the
foreground.

OPPOSITE, MIDDLE
Butterflyfish are almost
always seen in pairs. Most
keep the same mate for life.

OPPOSITE, BOTTOM
Moray eels are cleaned by
trusting fish and shrimp.
Their open mouths may look
aggressive, but don't be put
off: this is how they breathe.

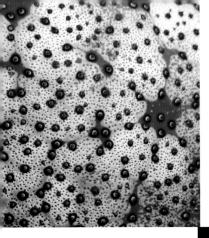

RIGHT
The walls at Tikehau can be literally alive with fish.

BELOW, RIGHT
Close encounters with grey and black-tip reef shark are guaranteed at Shark Hole.

ABOVE
A close-up of the beautifully patterned basket star.

OPPOSITE
Inquisitive Napoleon wrasse appear on nearly every dive.

RIGHT
The reef's craggy surface provides endless hidden vantage points for predators such as lionfish, scorpionfish and stonefish.

Almost as good is a site without a name right on the edge of Tuheiva Pass. Again, you'll discover vast fields of perfect hard coral – surely this is what all the world's reefs looked like before pollution and global warming. This is an easy dive, as always to a maximum of 100 ft, and you'll find countless lionfish hiding in the overhangs, some truly enormous stonefish wedged into impossible nooks, the ever-present Napoleon wrasse, the occasional hammerhead and a plethora of multi-coloured fish. Green morays are in abundance – it's not uncommon to see four or five at a time – but watch out if you're looking for a handhold on dead coral as these creatures possess the unfortunate combination of poor eyesight and sharp teeth.

In good weather you can explore the open sea just behind the hotel (although this is difficult to get to), while on a rising tide you can go on a fast drift dive through Tuheiva Pass; the latter is a must, as it brings with it all manner of life including manta ray and hammerheads. This is remote, unspoilt diving where anything can turn up, and drifting over acres of virgin coral in translucent waters, knowing there is no one else for miles, adds an edge to every dive.

Independent since 1821, the Republic of Costa Rica is Central America's jewel of stability, the most settled of the often somewhat troubled nations in the region. Located between Nicaragua and Panama, Costa Rica's two coastlines border the waters of the Caribbean and Pacific respectively, while in between lie some truly beautiful rainforests as well as a string of volcanoes. A number of these are still active; Arenal volcano in particular, a two-hour drive from the Papagayo Peninsula, provides an almost nightly firework display.

If you have already explored the best of Central America's Caribbean shore to the east, the west coast will give you a totally different experience, at least from a dive perspective. The narrow strip that connects the two Americas also separates two totally different marine habitats. The Pacific's nutrient-rich waters are wilder and cooler than those of the Caribbean, but they attract a blizzard of sea life; washing up from the south, they also bathe the Galapagos. You almost wonder whether the country's Spanish settlers had early access to scuba gear when they named it the 'Rich Coast'.

Nowhere represents this better than the Papagayo Peninsula, which lets you access it all in style. A sliver of land in the northwest corner of one of Costa Rica's least developed areas, it is home to the country's first truly five-star resort, the Four Seasons Peninsula Papagayo.

The 2,400-acre Papagayo Peninsula is part of a giant, government-backed development project on Costa Rica's Pacific coast. One day it will be peppered with resorts, but for the moment the Four Seasons has this shore all to itself, occupying its finest location. Years ago this was virgin forest; nowadays howler monkeys steal balls from the Arnold Palmer golf course and iguanas dice with the hotel's immaculate SUVs.

papagayo peninsula

RESORT four seasons peninsula papagayo

From the airport of Liberia, a 30-minute drive takes you to what looks to be the entrance to the hotel's grounds, announced by a stand of perfect palms. In fact this is the gateway to the peninsula. For five miles a brick road winds between forest and fairway until you reach the hub of the resort, flanked by a beach on either side. Of the two, the rather enthusiastically named Playa Blanca is not *blanca* at all, but rather 'greya'; Playa Virador is an altogether better bet. Both, however, offer calm, protected swimming.

Apparently designed to look like the lip of a terracotta pot, with rooms inspired by the shape of an armadillo, some may quibble with the resort's architectural aesthetic. Nonetheless, it is certainly different and successfully blends in with its surroundings.

The 123 rooms are arranged in three large wings, while the more upscale lodgings and suites are scattered in clusters on the hillside. The standard rooms are generous in size and beautifully furnished, featuring a typically faultless Four Seasons bed decked with fabulous linens, a spacious bathroom and a sort of inside–outside sitting room protected by an almost invisible mosquito screen. It is worth paying extra to stay on one of the upper floors, as the views are spectacular; lower down you have only a glimpse of water.

at a glance

Airport	Liberia
Airlines	American Airlines, Continental Airlines, Delta Airlines, United Airlines
Transfer time	45 mins by car from Liberia
Rooms	163 rooms and suites (all air-conditioned)
Staff ratio	4
Activities	Golf, nature tours, fishing, sailing, kayaking, rainforest canopy tours, white-water rafting, surfing, children's programmes, tennis, gym, spa, swimming pools
Services	Television, internet, room service
Children	All ages
Power type	2-pin flat
Currency	Costa Rican colon, US dollar
GMT	-6
Booking	www.diveinstyle.com

The three restaurants are overseen by the incredibly attentive staff; nothing is too much trouble. Breakfast is served in the brasserie, lunch either there or by the pool at Congos, and dinner at either of these, with the added option of elegant Italian restaurant Mare. The MAP (Modified American Plan) rate offers a good deal, though be sure to have the rules fully explained. Argentinian night at Congos is a particular treat, with a constant stream of fabulous barbecued meat and fish, guaranteed to satisfy anyone's appetite.

There is plenty to do, with special programmes for kids. For instance, expeditions to different rainforests give you a chance to see howler monkeys and scarlet macaws (though skip the 'skywalk' day excursion), while the resort offers a nonstop flow of activities, from Pilates to surfing and white-water rafting. Staying here, you benefit from all the service, style and comfort that has come to be synonymous with the Four Seasons name, along with distinctive architecture set against a stunning natural backdrop. Accommodation of this quality, in previously the poorest and most untouched part of Costa Rica, is an achievement in itself.

Diving at the Four Seasons Peninsula Papagayo is simplicity itself. Run by an American family, Diving Safaris is a 15-minute boat ride across the bay, not that you will ever have to visit. At 9 a.m. you leave for a two-tank dive from Playa Blanca, the hotel's own beach, and the team is always on time.

DIVE CENTER

A small boat takes you from the beach's edge to one of Diving Safaris' fleet of five boats. Though simple, the vessels are perfectly comfortable and fine for their task, especially considering that most of the dive sites are close by. The only exceptions are the Bat and Catalinas Islands, both of which are really day trips, but not to worry – Diving Safaris are equipped with the right boats to deal with longer journeys.

Only basic refreshments are offered on the boat, usually water, fruit and biscuits. But unless you go on a day trip, you normally return to the Four Seasons by 1 p.m., which leaves you plenty of time to have lunch at the resort.

The dive guides more than make up for any shortcomings in the food department, always doing their utmost to show you the best of the local exotics. As for your gear, you don't have to worry about it; they rig it, swap bottles after the first dive, then take it all away; the following day you find it on the boat, rinsed and ready to go.

Diving Safaris run Bubblemaker courses for kids in the hotel pool, and every Friday they also host an introduction to scuba for adults. It's a perfect opportunity to get hooked.

at a glance

Boats	25 ft+ (wet/dry, covered)
Group size	6
Instructors	5
Languages	English, Spanish
Courses	All PADI
Children	12+
Other	Nitrox and rebreathers (24 hrs notice), some food and drink, gear prep and wash down, private charters
Website	www.costaricadiving.net

If you're bent on seeing coral, then the diving off Papagayo is not for you; the same goes for the Galapagos and much of this eastern part of the Pacific. If, on the other hand, you're after some amazing marine life, you won't be disappointed – Papagayo is a bit like a junior Galapagos. This is the finest diving on Central America's Pacific coast, with the exception of the Cocos Islands, a few hundred miles offshore and only reachable by live-aboard.

ABOVE
There is no shortage of schooling fish, perhaps because of the lack of commercial fishing.

DIVING

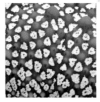

The sites near Papagayo host some fantastic sea life. Before diving Papagayo the seahorse and the harlequin clown shrimp had proved elusive. On the first dive at Virador, not only did they show up, but they brought company: arrestingly beautiful sea urchins, eagle ray, devil ray, jewel moray, snowflake moray, loggerhead turtle, scorpionfish, milkfish and vast schools of grunts.

Further afield, you are virtually guaranteed a close encounter with large bull shark at the famous Bat Islands. At any of the sites, you stand a genuine chance of losing your diving buddy in a flurry of fish. The water may not be perfectly clear and the underwater landscape could be more striking, but the marine life here is simply exceptional.

The water temperature and visibility are varied. For the best overall conditions, it's best to dive during the summer wet season, when visibility is up to 70 ft. But if you want to try to see killer whales, the huge Pacific manta ray or whale shark, then you will probably want to don a 5mm wetsuit and come when the water is cooler. If you can't bear the thought of a live-aboard, the diving nirvanas of the Cocos and Galapagos Islands are out of reach. Luckily, Papagayo comes close to the experience, while still allowing you to sleep in one of the best hotel beds in the world.

at a glance

Local sites	22
Level	Easy to advanced
Visibility	20–40 ft (December–March), 20–70 ft (April–November)
Must-dives	Virador, Bat Islands, Catalinas Islands
Snorkelling	Average from Playa Blanca, good from dive boat
Wetsuits	3mm in summer, 5mm in winter
Coral	Poor
Marine life	Harlequin clown shrimp, seahorse, jewel and zebra moray, bull and whale shark, eagle, devil and manta ray, schools of cownose ray, ridley, green and leatherback turtle, large schools of grunt, spade and jackfish, frogfish, pilot, humpback and killer whale
Other	Day trips, night dives, hyperbaric chamber (1.5 hrs), marine park at Bat Islands

OPPOSITE TOP, LEFT TO RIGHT
Snowflake moray, for once out of their lairs and on the hunt; seahorses are normally hard to find but have made their homes on a number of local reefs; the stunning but shy zebra moray, one of the more snake-like of the species, and common in the Catalinas Islands.

OPPOSITE, MAIN PICTURE
The extraordinary harlequin clown shrimp eat only starfish, a sort of living larder. They gorge on them for weeks, clinging on and feasting from the tube feet in.

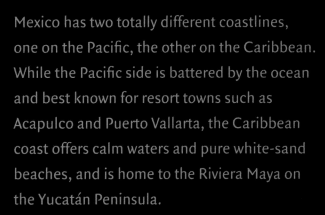

Mexico has two totally different coastlines, one on the Pacific, the other on the Caribbean. While the Pacific side is battered by the ocean and best known for resort towns such as Acapulco and Puerto Vallarta, the Caribbean coast offers calm waters and pure white-sand beaches, and is home to the Riviera Maya on the Yucatán Peninsula.

Cancún, the peninsula's main city, is the jumping-off point for the coast. A thriving metropolis dedicated to hedonistic delights, Cancún has become a byword for mass spring break and is dominated by tacky Aztec-themed high-rise hotels; what must once have been one of the most beautiful beaches in the Caribbean is now overrun by bars, nightclubs and casinos. Other towns nearby have followed suit: Tulum and Playa del Carmen, for instance, are famous for hosting droves of roaming students who go there to party.

It's hard to believe, but just 30 minutes south of Cancún you can find stylish luxury accommodation in practically untouched surroundings. Set in an ecological reserve and close to Mayan ruins, Hotel Maroma epitomizes the best the peninsula has to offer. The resort is so low-profile that most taxi drivers haven't even heard of it. Luckily directions aren't an issue: when you arrive at the airport, you're immediately whisked away in an immaculate air-conditioned 4 x 4. And once you get to Maroma, you won't have to worry about a thing.

The brainchild of architect José Luis Moreno, Hotel Maroma Resort and Spa nestles within a 500-acre coconut plantation blessed with a secluded bay and the finest white-sugar sand beach on the Riviera Maya. Although the property has changed hands and is now part of the Orient Express group, the hotel remains true to Moreno's vision. What's more, tight controls mean Maroma still enjoys the best and least-developed strip of real estate on Mexico's Caribbean coast.

yucatán peninsula

HOTEL

hotel maroma resort and spa

The road leading to Maroma is typically low-key. Leaving behind the manicured lawns and palm-lined avenues of other hotels, you turn off onto a mile-long track of sand and gravel through an ecological reserve of natural jungle. Finally you arrive at the oasis that is Maroma, and from the moment you enter the grounds you are made to feel welcome by the warm, genuine smiles of the staff. Maroma itself covers some 20 acres and unfolds as a series of intimate spaces. At its core is the beachside dining room, beyond which lies the tranquil main pool. The southern end of the resort hosts more recent additions to the complex, including a fitness room, spa and dive shop; the only minor downside is a nearby low-built resort but there's so much space you'll hardly notice.

Despite all the improvements and recent additions, including the Sian Nau plunge pool suites, the resort has managed to ensure that about 70 per cent of the rooms have ocean views, but I still feel an affinity for rooms 1–4 due to the particular intimacy and privacy they afford. The architectural style is a blend of both Mayan and Moorish, with soaring roofs in local wood; rough white-plaster walls, bamboo-strip shutters and tiled floors define the interiors. Each room gives onto its own spacious terrace, where a traditional Mexican hammock hangs ready to lull you into a siesta.

at a glance

Airport	Cancún International
Airlines	Aeroméxico, American Airlines, Continental Airlines, Delta Airlines, US Air, United Airways
Transfer time	30 mins by car
Rooms	65 rooms and suites and 1 villa (all air-conditioned)
Staff ratio	3
Activities	Hobie Cats, kayaking, Mayan ruins, windsurfing, sunset cruises, fishing, golf, horseriding, tennis, gym, yoga, swimming pools, spa
Services	Internet, shared television, room service
Other	Mobile phones
Children	16+
Power type	2-pin flat
Currency	Mexican peso (US dollar widely accepted)
GMT	-6
Booking	www.diveinstyle.com

Wherever you sleep, you're never more than a few steps away from the palapa-lined beach. And what a beach: two miles of perfect white powder, gently descending to the calm, protected waters of the bay. An inviting array of luxury beach furniture, including comfy chairs, loungers and large daybeds strewn with oversized cushions, ensures you'll want to stay put. And why shouldn't you? Say the word and you'll be brought everything from breakfast and lunch to a romantic torch-lit supper. You could spend your whole stay on the beach and not have to lift a finger.

If you can tear yourself away from the sand, it's worth venturing to Puerto Aventuras, a small town 40 minutes south of Maroma and probably the only place in the world where you'll have the chance to swim with dolphins, sting rays and manatees at the same time. You're also free to explore the magical Mayan ruins of Tulum or Chichen Itza, ride a horse through the jungle, go deep-sea fishing or play golf.

Where you eat is up to you with three restaurants to choose from, but there are few places better than the main terrace. Just on the beach's edge, this is where you'll find the open-air dining area shaded by soaring palms, albeit somewhat denuded by the recent hurricanes, and with views onto the multi-hued ocean. The dress code is basically casual, but while in the day informality rules, at night a little more elegance is required. The food at lunch and dinner is 'Yucatán contemporary cuisine'; breakfast is a particular treat – fresh juices and homemade jams from the exotic local fruit, as well as creamy pancakes with cinnamon syrup.

No description of Maroma would be complete without a mention of the Temazcal, an ancient Aztec ritual of spiritual and physical cleansing carried out here every evening. It is not for the faint-hearted: you descend into a dark, semi-buried steam room while you listen to the sound of traditional incantations. It's certainly an experience, but for the non-masochistic, the amazing 7,000 ft^2 spa with everything from Botox to body rubs is a far better bet.

One of the best things about Maroma is that even when it's fully booked, you'll wonder where all the guests went. The beachside dining room is rarely more than half full, there's always space under a palapa and never a crowd at the bar – or anywhere for that matter. Regardless of when you come, the place feels wonderfully empty.

The colourful team who ran this tiny diving outfit has moved on, and while perhaps their unique character will be missed, other aspects of the service have definitely improved, certainly regarding the equipment.

DIVE CENTER

The diving here is highly personalized. Most dives are for only two to four guests, so you generally turn up at an appointed time of your own choosing. Departures tend to be around 9 to 9.15 a.m., when you take a short wade out to the boat, a now less colourful but far more comfortable and practical 30-ft RIB. While it still offers a limited amount of cover, this isn't a problem as all the dive sites are under ten minutes away; alternative arrangements can be made if you want to take a day trip further afield.

The center has now completely re-equipped with all new Scubapro gear and also offers computers for hire; I still recommend bringing your own mask – no dive operation ever seems to offer anything better than adequate. Common sense dictates that you take any computers and underwater cameras back to your room, but otherwise the center takes care of your equipment throughout your stay. Your gear awaits you when you board, rigged and ready for diving, and is rinsed and dried for your next dive once you're done for the day.

A private 'guided' snorkel is to be recommended, a service that seems to be becoming more popular worldwide and if you want to make the transition to diving there is no better place than in one of Maroma's heated pools.

at a glance

Boats	30 ft (wet, partially covered)
Group size	4
Instructors	1
Languages	English, Spanish, French, Portuguese
Courses	PADI
Children	16+
Other	Computer hire, drinks, nitrox and rebreathers (by prior arrangement), gear prep and wash down, private charters

The variety of the diving here is outstanding, and there are no fewer than 15 sites within ten minutes of the dive center. There's something for everyone: beginners can explore the thriving shallow reef ledges and their tiny drop-offs, while experienced thrill-seekers can ride the famous Maroma current and dive the *cenotes* or inland sinkholes.

ABOVE
The ungainly arrow crab seeks
safety in the arms of an anemone.

DIVING

There are no real wall dives, only easy shallow dives offering mini-walls of about 10 ft between plateaus, located at just 40–50 ft. These are home to dense, thriving ecosystems; fan and large brain corals are especially common. Schools of grunts, rubias and the occasional rare toadfish gravitate here, and don't seem to mind the presence of divers so long as you keep your breathing slow. Spotted and green morays abound, although the latter are easier to see on night dives.

Another good dive for beginners is at New Reef. The site is a band of shallow coral some 40 ft wide, with plenty of canyons and overhangs that are ideal for cruising at your own pace. Sea life abounds: you'll see yellow rays, stingrays, lobsters, parrotfish, squirrelfish, grouper and grey angelfish, among other common reef species.

If you want bigger fish, then you'll need a bit more experience. Turtle Plain is a plateau at about 100 ft, which is constantly swept by the powerful Maroma current. Relatively barren and dotted with hundreds of giant sponges bent double by the relentless current, this is where large green and hawksbill turtles come to feed; while you struggle to hang on to a rock or sponge, they seem to glide effortlessly against the flow of water.

at a glance

Local sites	15
Level	Easy to advanced
Visibility	70 ft+
Must-dives	Cenotes, Maroma drift dive
Snorkelling	Good on house reef
Wetsuits	3mm
Coral	Very good
Marine life	Large green and hawksbill turtle, terminal phase parrotfish, bull, nurse and whale shark, dolphin, manatee, toadfish
Other	Day trips during whale-shark season, night dives, hyperbaric chamber at Playa del Carmen (15 mins)

OPPOSITE, TOP
The coral reefs of the Yucatán
Peninsula host over 500 species
of fish, including rubia.

OPPOSITE, MAIN PICTURE
The Grand Cenote, a cavern
dive accessible even to novice
divers. It's difficult to believe
this is actually under water.

OPPOSITE, MIDDLE
Jaws agape, a grouper hovers
at a cleaning station.

OPPOSITE, BOTTOM
Most species of grouper
flush or colour up when
being cleaned.

LEFT
The shallow, protected waters of
New Reef give you the opportunity
for long, easy dives.

BELOW, LEFT
While a turtle floats effortlessly,
grazing in the Maroma's strong
currents, a diver struggles to
maintain station.

Those looking for an adrenaline rush can do no better than the
Maroma drift dive. You're dropped off in deep water and descend to
nearly 130 ft, where you pick up the current and fly past turtles along
the top of a 6,000-ft wall. In the gloom you can make out what at first
seem to be lost Napoleon wrasse. In fact, these are giant terminal-
phase parrotfish, whose brilliant colours grow dazzling as you near
them; they pass all too quickly as you are swept along by the current.

Further afield, manatee and dolphin await you at Puerto Aventuras,
while from June to September you can swim or snorkel with whale
sharks at Holbox Island; this is a must, especially now the resort
has arranged private trips. The hotel also offers a day trip to two
remarkable cenotes: Grande Cenote, near the Mayan ruin of Tulum,
followed by Dos Ojos Cenote.

Although you can snorkel at Grande Cenote, it needs to be dived for
full effect. More cavern diving than cave diving, it offers seemingly
endless visibility: as you drop into the water, you're struck first by
its coolness relative to the sea, and then by its pure transparency.
Following your guide, you 'fly' your way through stalactites and
stalagmites; in between caverns, you catch magical glimpses of
sunlight shafts through the deep turquoise water.

The other less crowded alternatives are the literally crystal clear
waters of Dos Ojos, complete with a genuine bat cave into which you
can surface during the dive. Again, this is all cavern diving so you are
always in sight of reassuring bright shafts of sunlight, although if
you are tempted by the safety lines disappearing into dark caves, the
team are qualified to help.

LEFT

There is no shortage of fish life, fed by the nutrient-rich currents.

RIGHT

Octopus can take on an amazing range of colours and textures in their quest for anonymity.

BELOW

The majestic eagle ray, a regular sight on the drop-off.

The Florida Keys are a lot like the Caribbean – except you can get here by car. It's worth the trip just for the drive. Made up of over 200 islands, 34 of which are inhabited, the Keys are linked by the scenic Overseas Highway (also known as US 1), 112 miles of single-lane road and 43 bridges spanning the endless turquoise waters. When you reach the end, you are closer to Havana than Miami.

If Henry Flagler had had his way, you could keep on driving. Until 1912 there was no connecting road to the Keys. But Flagler, a tycoon and railroad developer, noticed that Key West was then the only deep-water port on the USA's southeastern coast. Hoping to take advantage of its proximity to the Panama Canal, he privately funded a causeway and railway connecting the islands and the mainland. He even got as far as building a seven-mile section towards Cuba before the Labour Day Hurricane of 1935, the strongest ever to hit the east coast, washed away most of his work.

The first of the Keys is Key Largo, where the roadside is littered with dive shops and quirky stores. Over a hundred miles down is colourful Key West, Hemingway's most famous haunt and the furthest south of all American cities, its deadpan spirit encapsulated by a famous local tombstone marked 'I told you I was sick'. But if you're looking for a luxury escape, the place to go lies in-between: Little Palm Island, just off Little Torch Key.

It's hardly surprising that the makers of *PT 109*, the classic movie about President Kennedy's wartime experiences, chose Little Palm Island to fool cinema-goers into thinking it was shot in the South Pacific. This is five acres of film-set perfection. Over 100 miles from Miami, the island is a short boat ride from the Keys' arterial road, but it seems a lifetime away.

florida

HOTEL little palm island

From a discreet reception lodge on Little Torch Key, a private 1930s-style motorboat transports you 10,000 miles in just ten minutes – or at least it seems that way. Once you are immersed in the stylish and luxurious world that is Little Palm Island, it is seriously difficult to believe you are still in Florida, let alone the US.

The first thing that strikes you is the island's luxuriant vegetation. Then you notice the constant sound of birdsong. Little Palm is home to the most incredible diversity of migrating birds you can imagine, including herons, egrets, hawks, parakeets, doves, pelicans and cormorants – it's like stepping into an outdoor aviary. Nowhere else in the Keys will you find this phenomenon, and even the Audubon Society for bird protection acknowledges that this is very special.

At the heart of the resort is an intimate palm-fringed pool, which is overlooked by the Palapa Bar, the restaurant, a cosy library and a boutique. All are housed in irregular single-storey, rough timber-clad structures that give the place the feel of a private house with outbuildings. It's easy to forget you're at a hotel.

A perfect white-sand path runs around the perimeter of the complex, and off this lie 28 raised, thatched-roof bungalow suites, all with

at a glance

Airport	Miami or Key West
Airlines	American Airlines, Continental Airlines, Delta Airlines, US Air
Transfer time	40 mins from Key West or 2.5 hrs from Miami by car, then 10 mins by boat
Rooms	28 rooms, 2 suites (all air-conditioned)
Staff ratio	4
Activities	Watersports, excursions to Key West, gym, spa, swimming pool
Services	Limited room service
Children	16+
Power type	2-pin flat
Currency	US dollar
GMT	-5
Booking	www.diveinstyle.com

ocean views, and all private. The sense of South Seas remoteness is taken further with no in-room telephones or televisions, a brave move in North America. The rooms feature vaulted ceilings, a bed draped in mosquito netting, a sitting room, whirlpool bathtubs, indoor and outdoor showers and a small private veranda. What's more, they are filled with generous touches such as your own personalized letter paper, a teddy bear on the bed and an open bar. It's like staying with a friend, only better.

The dining room is perched on a small sandy point, and it's up to you whether you eat in the air-conditioned interior, the shade overlooking the beach, or on the water's edge. Dinner is also served on the sand by the light of guttering torches, so you can watch the sun sink and the pelicans dive as you sample the sensational food. Just when you think things can't get any better, a rare Key deer, an endangered species, nuzzles up to you for food. By now you will have appreciated that Little Palm is something of an eco-sanctuary.

That said, the beach looks better than it is. The Keys aren't far from the Bahamas, but they are not blessed with the same great beaches, so don't expect Turks and Caicos-style swimming. Instead you can try something a bit different: lie back on the boardwalk or at one of the secluded spots that dot the island, or take a small boat out to explore the mangroves; if you're lucky you will find manatees, which come to Little Palm for the sea grass, their favourite food. If you want to go further afield, the dive center offers eco-kayaking tours to the Great White Heron National Wildlife Refuge.

This is a superbly run resort, with a staff-to-guest ratio more in keeping with the Far East than the West. Its location is unbeatable, the wildlife amazing and the environment unusual – it couldn't be further from your mainstream American hotel. There are no cars here; the only sounds are the splash of fishing pelicans and the occasional passing boat. It's the perfect base for exploring the Keys, and there is no place better for discovering the area's best diving.

Located in Little Palm Island's sheltered harbour, where Hollywood's *PT 109* used to dock, this dive center is just behind the spa and, like everything else, a short walk from any of the rooms. It may be small, but it has an excellent range of equipment that is regularly replaced. The whole operation is designed to make diving here as painless as possible.

DIVE CENTER

The immaculate 28-ft *Island Girl* can carry up to 14 people, but given the size of the resort its full capacity is rarely put to the test; in any case, dive groups are kept to a maximum of six. It's quite a wet boat, so it's a good idea to carry a dry bag.

Since sites such as Looe Key and the *Adolphus Busch* are very close, there is no need for catered day trips. Nonetheless, the boat always carries cold drinks and plenty of towels. If you feel chilly after a long dive (you can easily spend 90 minutes underwater at Looe Key), you even get to wear a long, lined waterproof overcoat that is guaranteed to keep you warm. This is one boat you will never get cold on, regardless of conditions – all eventualities have been covered.

The center also makes it easy for you to dive further afield. If you have time to take in the *Thunderbolt* wreck up in Marathon, you will be driven 30 minutes or so north to the small but perfectly organized Deep Blue Dive Center. This runs you out to the site some 20 minutes away, and then to a second, shallower dive. If you want to make a day of it, on your way back you can stop for lunch at one of the many restaurants overlooking the ocean. In short, this is a quality set-up and a seamless extension to the resort.

at a glance

Boats	28 ft+ (wet, covered)
Group size	6
Instructors	2
Languages	English
Courses	All PADI
Children	16+
Other	Nitrox, rebreathers, drinks, gear prep and wash down, private charters, underwater scooter hire

There are two types of diving here. The first is gentle, shallow and very easy – ideal for beginners. The second is exciting, deep wreck diving, often swept by currents, and is only for more advanced divers. Regardless of your experience, this is excellent diving with something for everyone.

ABOVE

The wrecks around Little Palm provide a haven for both predator and prey. The barracuda seem particularly well fed.

DIVING

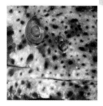

Named after the unfortunate H.M.S. *Looe* which sank on the reef in 1742, Looe Key was designated a marine reserve in 1981. Only a 20-minute ride from the resort, it is home to some of the most spectacular spur and groove coral formations anywhere on the Keys. What's more, the turquoise waters are so clear that you'd be forgiven for thinking you were in the Bahamas. It is difficult to get much deeper than about 30 ft, so this is an ideal place for both learning to dive and doing qualification dives.

at a glance

Local sites	30+
Level	Easy to advanced
Visibility	80 ft May–October, 30 ft November–April
Must-dives	Looe Key, *Adolphus Busch*, *Thunderbolt*
Snorkelling	Very good from dive boat
Wetsuits	3mm
Coral	Good
Marine life	Bottlenose dolphin, eagle ray, black-tip, bull, nurse and reef shark, Goliath grouper, green and spotted moray, tarpon, manatee
Other	Day trips, night dives, wreck dives, marine park

While the coral is healthy, the most remarkable thing about Looe Key is that it is absolutely bursting with fish life; it's as though word has got out among fish circles that the area is protected. You'll see schools of grunt, porgy, sergeant major and goatfish, and if you're lucky, you'll be blessed with the brief but beautiful sight of a resident school of midnight parrotfish; like a scene from an underwater Hitchcock movie, these descend from nowhere in a cloud, gorging briefly on the coral before rushing on.

But that's not all. There are also grey, French and queen angelfish, barracuda, green and spotted moray. If you look under the ledges and overhangs, you may find an accommodating Goliath grouper, and looking up you might spot a reef shark or eagle ray. All this is

OPPOSITE, CLOCKWISE FROM TOP LEFT

Schools of yellowtail are plentiful; the fish life in Looe Key marine park is some of the richest in the coastal waters of the USA; like most of their species, grey angelfish mate for life; the Florida Keys are home to an abundance of wrecks, a playground for both novices and more experienced divers.

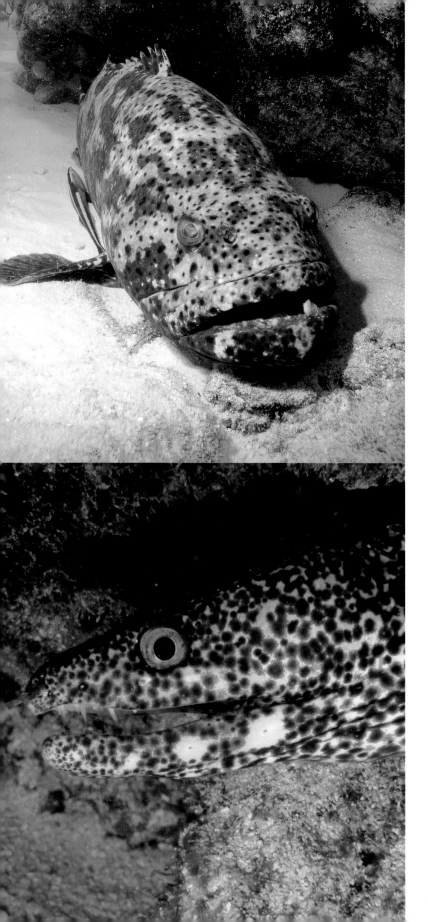

amazing to see given you are in the USA, and one of the benefits of this dive is that it is so shallow that you can spend forever underwater just watching the sea life go by. Granted, the diving can't compare to somewhere like Indonesia or the Great Barrier Reef in terms of variety. But it is still incredibly rewarding, and beginners will see more underwater action here than at many better-known dive spots.

If you're looking for more of a challenge, then the wreck dives are for you. You can head to either the *Adolphus Busch*, a 25-minute boat ride, or the *Thunderbolt* at Marathon Key, a bit further out but definitely worth the trip. These sites have varying visibility and are quite deep at around 100 ft, so to get the most out of them it's best to breathe nitrox, especially given the strict local diving guidelines.

The *Adolphus Busch* lies beneath 108 ft of water, while the 188-ft *Thunderbolt* sits upright at 115 ft. The latter was once used for studying lightning, as its name suggests; a balloon on a steel cable was floated into thunderstorms to encourage strikes. At both of these sites, you will find the reclusive giants, seriously big Goliath groupers; these are somewhat timid as they were once nearly wiped out by speargun-fishing, but they are now enjoying a comeback thanks to their new-found status as a protected species. In addition, chrome-plated 100lb tarpon glint in the water, jack hunt the droves of glassfish, and large barracuda seem to think they own the wrecks. Even if you've dived other, more spectacular sites in other parts of the world, this is wonderful diving, and it's one of the greatest and most surprising perks of staying at Little Palm.

The monogamous grey angelfish is normally very approachable.

The *Thunderbolt*, one of the finest wreck dives in the Keys, finished her days as an experiment to determine the effects of lightning on ships. A tethered balloon from this very spool was floated into thunderstorms to attract lightning.

The aptly named four-eye butterflyfish uses its extra 'eyes' to confuse predators.

Belize has come late to tourism. A British colony until 1981 with a disputed Guatemalan border, the country only really achieved political stability in 1998. As a consequence, much of it is still untouched: there are jaguars and rainforests in the hinterland, and you'll find virgin reefs off the coast. Thankfully the government has committed to protecting these natural resources, linking up with privately funded conservation groups.

If you believe the magazines, the place to go is San Pedro. But aside from a few Disneyesque stingray and shark-feeding dives, you're bound to be disappointed: the reefs have been stripped clean by the almost annual hurricanes. You'll have better luck further south. Two hours away are the fabled Blue Hole and the Turneffe Islands; the former is interesting, but the latter offer some of the best diving in the Caribbean. However, accommodation is limited: if you're willing to accept the time penalty, you can stay at the small but chic Mata Chica in San Pedro, but five hours of daily travel is hardly diving in style.

You would do better to head even further south, where you'll come to the ever-evolving Turtle Inn on the Placencia Peninsula. Aside from plentiful year-round sea life, in season you are guaranteed to find whale shark just an hour off the coast: this is the only place in the world where marine biologists have figured out why and exactly when these gentle behemoth turn up. For land-lovers, there's also hiking in the beautiful interior. It's an unbeatable combination.

In 2002, there was both good news and bad news for Turtle Inn. The bad news was that Hurricane Iris had almost levelled it. And the good news? Hurricane Iris had almost levelled it! This small resort was the brainchild of film director Francis Ford Coppola, and when nature presented him with a clean canvas, he used the opportunity to create a whole new resort.

placencia peninsula

HOTEL turtle inn

The approach to Turtle Inn stands out thanks to its immaculate lush green lawns. Given that the land was practically stripped bare in 2002, Coppola and his team have done a remarkable job of restoring it – you would have no idea of its recent history. The nearest town is sleepy Placencia, which lies on a peninsula a 30-minute flight south of Belize City. Regularly serviced by efficient local airline Tropic Air, this long, narrow strip of land juts out from the coast just inches above sea level, and is sandwiched between two bodies of water: on one side it fronts the open ocean, while on the other it borders a sheltered lagoon that is home to everything from manatees to 18-ft crocodiles.

Built under soaring thatched roofs, the resort features a blend of Mayan and Balinese influences. This theme runs throughout the design: carved stone reliefs, antique-style painted doors, ornate timber friezes, stone paths lined with candles... Even if you didn't know the owner's identity, you can't help but feel there's something theatrical about it all; it's a bit like an impeccable stage set.

The rooms are either directly on the beach or a 30-second walk from it. Each is a free-standing, thatched-roofed raised hut, with a generous screened porch, a spacious sitting area, a comfortable bedroom and a queen-sized bed. While the bed size is surprising – there is plenty of

at a glance

Airport	Placencia via Belize City
Airlines	American, Continental, Delta or US Air, then Tropic Air/Maya Island Air to Placencia
Transfer time	3 mins by car
Rooms	25 (none air-conditioned)
Staff ratio	3+
Activities	Watersports, fishing, jaguar spotting, rainforest, swimming pools, spa
Services	Internet, room service
Other	Mobile phones allowed
Children	All ages
Power type	2-pin flat
Currency	Belizean dollar (US dollar widely accepted)
GMT	-6
Booking	www.diveinstyle.com

room – this is not an oversight, as Coppola explains: 'If you are here alone you don't need a king, and if you are here with someone you love, you shouldn't want one!'

No two rooms are exactly the same: you can choose from the Honeymoon Cottage, the Chinese Matrimonial Suite, the Pavilion House, and the two-bedroom villas (ideal for families or friends). All have a distinctly Balinese feel to them, with their high roofs, carved doors, timber surrounds, and stone carvings and statues. Although they are not air-conditioned, they are surprisingly cool thanks to quiet but effective ceiling fans; invariably ocean-front rooms or the new rooms around the private triangular pool are the preferred.

Although Belize's tourist board insists that Placencia has some of the country's best beaches, there is neither powder-white sand nor clear turquoise water. While the excellent staff go to great lengths to make up for this by endlessly raking the beach of seaweed, the best options for swimming are either the beautiful circular main pool or the new triangular one; Coppola does not do rectangles.

Meals are usually served in the Mare Restaurant, which looks out onto the pool and ocean. The ever-obliging staff will also arrange dinner for you on the beach, while for lunch you can eat at the sand-floored Laughing Fish Bar on the water's edge. The chef uses local ingredients, including organic produce from sister resort Blancaneaux Lodge, and he has created a menu with a distinctly Italian edge to it, reflecting Coppola's roots. If you fancy a change and want to eat 'locale', Auntie Luba's, a two-minute stroll, is the newest addition overlooking the lagoon.

Turtle Inn is very special. True to its owner's vision, the resort has retained its own individual character, and it looks set to stay that way. You may not find perfect white-sand beaches, but you are surrounded by nature, both above and beneath the water: manatees, rainforests, waterfalls and the world's only jaguar reserve, not to mention some incredible marine life, including whale shark. There is no better place to discover all this and more.

A two-minute walk brings you to Tides Dive Center, situated on the lagoon en route to Turtle Inn's spa. The shop sells T-shirts and a few dive-related goods, and is extremely well equipped – all you should bring is your own mask. Before diving, it's crucial to ask if there are any *pica pica* in the water. These are microscopic larval jellyfish, and if they're around, the shop's sunscreen-cum-repellent is a serious mandatory buy.

DIVE CENTER

The boats are all virtually new, the latest being a fast 46-footer designed to get you to the sites quickly. Although you are sheltered by the reef, the weather can pick up and the crossing can be a little bumpy. Take along a waterproof bag if you have a camera or anything else you want to keep dry.

The center's hookah breathing system allows non-divers to descend to a depth of 25 ft; air is provided from a floating compressor. This is used at Laughingbird Cay and is an ideal stepping stone to becoming a qualified diver – something you can also do here.

The hotel beach is not of much interest for snorkellers unless there are manatees around or perfect visibility, so joining one of the dive trips is a must. The Cays are great for snorkelling, but what's really exceptional is the reality-adjusting whale shark dive or snorkel.

Most diving is organized as day trips, either to the inner atolls, 30 minutes away, or the barrier reef, an hour-long journey. With the exception of the whale shark dive, your surface interval is spent enjoying lunch on the white-sand beach of some palm-fringed, atom-sized island. The ever-smiling dive crew change your tanks while you indulge, and look after your gear at the end of the day.

at a glance

Boats	46 and 26 ft+ (wet, partially covered)
Group size	6
Instructors	2
Languages	English, Spanish
Courses	All PADI
Children	12+
Other	Computer and underwater camera hire, food and drinks, wash down, private charters, dive shop, hookah diving (helmet diving – no tanks, no experience necessary)

Many people go to northern and central Belize to dive, but what those areas offer cannot come close to the experience of diving Gladden Spit. A marine park since 2001 thanks to a groundbreaking initiative by Friends of Nature and the Belizean government, this is a site where, at the right time of year, diving or snorkelling with whale shark is virtually guaranteed.

DIVING

Whereas in the past Honduran fishermen would come to Gladden Spit to net the snapper that congregate here, nowadays the area is carefully monitored and protected in consultation with local dive operators. Boats are allotted a dedicated time slot to ensure that the whale sharks' natural behaviour is interrupted as little as possible, a policy that also offers a better experience for the diver. These are 'blue water' dives where you swim along at 60–70 ft: the bottom barely visible, with little to orientate yourself apart from the occasional dark shadow of a large bull shark or a blue marlin. If you come at the wrong time you may see nothing, but in the right season after the full moon, the diving here is literally unbelievable.

Fishermen always knew that something special was going on here: they regularly filled their small boats with a seemingly unending supply of line-caught snapper, and were constantly surrounded by whale shark. But it wasn't until a marine biologist came to dive that the link between the two species became clear. Enormous schools of snapper come here to spawn, producing billions of microscopic eggs that appear as great white clouds; this is what attracts the whale shark which come here to feed, their vast mouths agape. These gentle giants, up to 50 ft long, will pass within inches of you; the first time you see one is an experience that stays with you forever.

at a glance

Local sites	12
Level	Easy to advanced
Visibility	50 ft inside reef, 100 ft outside reef
Must-dives	Gladden Spit, Glovers Reef
Snorkelling	Very good from dive boat
Wetsuits	3mm
Coral	Very good
Marine life	Whale shark, huge schools of snapper and jack, nassau, tiger, black and yellowfin grouper, sharptail eel, bull, nurse and lemon shark, loggerhead and leatherback turtle, bottlenose and spotted dolphin, Goliath grouper, manatee, toadfish
Other	Day trips, night dives, wreck dive, marine park

ABOVE
Large schools of jackfish are just one of the highlights of the blue-water whale shark dives.

OPPOSITE
The central and southern Belizean reefs are home to a rich tapestry of marine life, including schools of sergeant major.

RIGHT
The loggerhead turtle is so slow-moving that it is always encrusted with marine growth.

ABOVE
Vast schools of spawning snapper rise from the depths – the moment that the whale shark have been waiting for.

RIGHT
The Belizean barrier reef is the second largest in the world, only exceeded by Australia's Great Barrier Reef.

Diving with whale shark is an incredible adventure, but while the experience cannot be exaggerated, this is not all that Belizean diving has to offer. Unlike northern Belize where the barrier reef hugs the coast off San Pedro, here it is some 30 miles away. In between lie various cays and atolls, where the corals are all in excellent health; visibility is somewhat limited compared to the barrier reef, but it's a true garden of soft waving fans.

Wall dives are the order of the day if you venture out to the barrier reef, the longest in the western hemisphere, which plummets here to 7,000 ft. Fish life abounds: you will find moray, dolphin, nudibranchs, Goliath grouper, manta ray, eagle ray, bull and lemon shark. There are also four species of turtle, including the rarer, slothful loggerhead.

Laughing Bird Cay, half an hour away from Turtle Inn, is one of only three *faros* or submerged atolls in the world. The site of short day trips and night dives, it is home to two rare toadfish, the white-spotted and white-lined. It is also well known for inquisitive lemon and nurse shark. Glovers Reef is more spectacular, with walls falling to 2,000 ft, although the trip requires calm seas. In short, this part of Belize will reward you with some truly amazing diving – surely the best in the Caribbean – and being in the water with whale shark is a true highlight.

Home to nearly 40 island countries, the Caribbean has no shortage of desirable destinations, so it's odd that great hotels and great diving seem to be almost mutually exclusive. On the one hand, head south to the ABC islands (Aruba, Bonaire, Curaçao) or north to the Cayman Islands and you'll find some exceptional diving, but the accommodation is disappointing. On the other hand, travel to better-known places such as Antigua, Jamaica or Barbados and you'll stay at fantastic resorts, but the diving simply isn't up to scratch.

The British Virgin Islands give you the best of both worlds. It was Columbus who first put them on the map: he sailed through here in 1493 on his second visit to the New World, and named the untouched islands Las Virgenes in reference to Saint Ursula and her 11,000 attendant virgins; such are the rights of discovery. Peter Island is at the epicenter of the area's wonderful dives, including the 19th-century RMS *Rhone*, widely recognized as the Caribbean's greatest wreck dive.

Step aboard the *Turks and Caicos Aggressor II* for something completely different: a snorkelling adventure with humpback whales, a truly life-changing experience. With the Turks and Caicos so near, it's also worth checking out Amanyara; located on the island of Providenciales, it offers that Caribbean rarity of great diving combined with world-class accommodation.

Peter Island offers the perfect solution for diving in the Caribbean. Privately owned and almost impossibly large, comprising 1,800 pristine acres fringed with endless white-sand beaches, it is located right next door to the very best diving in the British Virgin Islands. The hotel first opened in the 1960s and gradually climbed its way upmarket. Today it has been revitalized as a true luxury resort.

peter island

HOTEL peter island

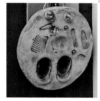

Taming and running an island of this size is not cheap; just building the harbour was a major undertaking. It's a good example of how to make a small fortune by starting off with a large one. First bought by Norwegian millionaire Peter Smedwig in the late 1960s, Peter Island was taken over in the following decade by two entrepreneurs who lavished a veritable fortune on it. Like many private islands, this one ended up absorbing cash like a black hole absorbs light – unfortunate for the owners, but as a guest you get to reap the benefits.

You might expect the British Virgin Islands to be lush and verdant, but they lack the necessary rainfall. Peter Island is no different. A bit like a monk's head, it is thick with vegetation along its cultivated fringe, but this thins once you leave the shoreline. The manicured perfection of the perimeter is thanks to an army of gardeners and an all-encompassing irrigation system: together this creates a botanical dream, with all kinds of exotic palms, bougainvillea and frangipani crowding the carefully swept borders.

The resort sits next door to its own marina, which is also where the pool, restaurant and bar look out towards Tortola. Nearby are the 32 Ocean View rooms, which back onto the marina and offer glimpses of the sea through a screen of palms; the rooms

at a glance

Airport	Beef Island Tortola via San Juan
Airlines	American Airlines
Transfer time	35 mins by boat
Rooms	52 rooms, plus villas (all air-conditioned)
Staff ratio	4+
Activities	Watersports, basketball, golf (off island), fishing, swimming pool, hiking, tennis, gym, spa
Services	Internet, telephone, heliport, room service (breakfast and dinner)
Other	Mobile phones allowed
Children	8+
Power type	2-pin flat
Currency	US dollar
GMT	-5
Booking	www.diveinstyle.com

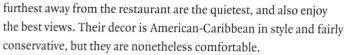

furthest away from the restaurant are the quietest, and also enjoy the best views. Their decor is American-Caribbean in style and fairly conservative, but they are nonetheless comfortable.

Your best bet for accommodation is a five-minute walk or a one-minute shuttle ride away. Here you'll find the 20 superb modern Beach Suites, which offer a generous sitting area, private terrace and vast bathroom with a spacious shower and bath for two. Better still, they give you captivating views over the ocean and neighbouring deserted islands, some opening onto an impeccably tended lawn, where you can relax in your own hammock.

In fact, the hammock is the emblem of Peter Island, and there are plenty more of them on the beach of Deadman's Bay. Nearly a mile long, it is a perfect white-powder crescent dotted with thatched huts and umbrellas. Unlike most beaches and bays in these islands, which tend to be crowded with charters, those on Peter Island are protected from uninvited guests; not only has the resort staked out its waters with buoys, but it has even gone to the extreme of setting aside a distant beach just for boats.

At the very end of Deadman's Beach is a truly world-class spa. Its unbeatable location overlooks a deserted white-sand cove, a favourite fishing spot for pelicans and home to what must be the finest snorkelling on the island. Even if you're not into spas, it's worth indulging in one of the excellent treatments just to gain access to the grounds. When you do, you can collapse into the hot tub and gaze out over the surf and the pelicans splashing in the shallows.

Until fairly recently, Peter Island had had the same chef for 30 years, surely a record for any hotel. New hands are in the kitchen but the food remains excellent, with international cuisine served at the open-air Deadman's Beach Grill and the air-conditioned Tradewinds Restaurant. The staff couldn't be friendlier, always stopping for a chat; you are treated more like a family friend than a hotel guest.

Peter Island is an upscale, manicured piece of the Caribbean. Not only does it keep getting better, but it has both the commitment and wherewithal to do so. Most importantly, while its design may not be as cutting-edge as at other resorts, its location is second to none.

Diving at Peter Island could not be easier. Two minutes from any of the rooms and you are at Paradise Watersports, right on the private harbour and just yards from the dive boat. Thanks to the island's amazing location there is no need for painfully early starts; the wreck of the RMS *Rhone*, the British Virgin Islands' most popular dive site, is just 15 minutes away, and you can depart at 9.30 a.m. after a delicious and leisurely breakfast.

DIVE CENTER

The small shop is stacked with equipment and even hires out digital underwater cameras. Although they prefer you to rig your own gear, all you have to do is ask and they will do this for you, as well as change your tanks for the second dive.

The boat is a wide, comfortable old 30-ft cruiser, ideally suited to her task, especially since all the sites are under 30 minutes away so there is no need for day trips; once again, you can't beat Peter Island as a location for diving.

If you are lucky, you will get to dive with Randy, who owns the dive shop. His experience of these seas is vast, and not only will he regale you with stories of large shark encounters while working with film crews out in the deep, but you will benefit from his tremendous underwater knowledge: he seems to notice everything, and his enthusiasm turns even the most average dive into a treat.

Once you return to the island, you can just dump your gear and make a beeline for lunch. They will rinse and look after the equipment, returning it to the boat for the afternoon dive or the next day. This small, highly attentive dive team offers excellent, personalized service that complements the resort to perfection.

at a glance

Boats	30 ft (dry, covered)
Group size	6+
Instructors	4
Languages	English
Courses	All PADI
Children	12+
Other	Computer and underwater camera hire, wash down, drinks, dive shop

The Virgin Islands rank at the top of many dive magazine polls, especially in the USA, and it's easy to see why. The islands are easy to reach, the seas sheltered, the locals friendly, and the choice of resorts huge. What's more, the diving is truly excellent, including spectacular wreck dives. There is an abundance of fish life, and the variety of sites offers something for both novice and more experienced divers.

DIVING

The protected waters of the islands are ideal for snorkelling or diving. Snorkellers should head for the Baths at Virgin Gorda: a collection of giant granite boulders, these form a series of spectacular pools that are perfect for exploring. Weather permitting, it's possible for divers to venture to the outer reefs where there is a chance of encountering bigger life, from large schools of horse-eyed jack and African pompano to rainbow runner and permit. There are also sightings of shark, including bull, great hammerhead, lemon, and even silky, dusky and Galapagos shark.

The reefs are in great shape, with forests of waving fans and soft corals. There is also fire coral, especially at Santa Monica Rock; it stings, so keep your hands to yourself. The dives are mostly spur and groove reefs falling away to a sandy floor, often punctuated with blennies and jawfish, garden eels waving back and forth and large stingray that seem to think they look inconspicuous covered in sand; keep a look out in the turtle grass as, aside from trumpetfish, just occasionally you might see the beautiful gold-spotted snake eel.

What people really come here for, however, are the wrecks. The RMS *Rhone* is one of the world's most famous wreck dives, and you should probably dive her at least twice. Moored off Peter Island during the

at a glance

Local sites	25
Level	Easy to advanced
Visibility	100 ft
Must-dives	RMS *Rhone*
Snorkelling	Good on house reef and from dive boat
Wetsuits	3mm
Coral	Very good
Marine life	Cobia, leopard and lettuce flatworm, eagle ray, gold-spotted snake eel, goldentail, viper, chain, spotted and green moray, reef, nurse, bull, great hammerhead, lemon and silky shark, humpback whale, tarpon, frogfish
Other	Night dives, wreck dives, marine park

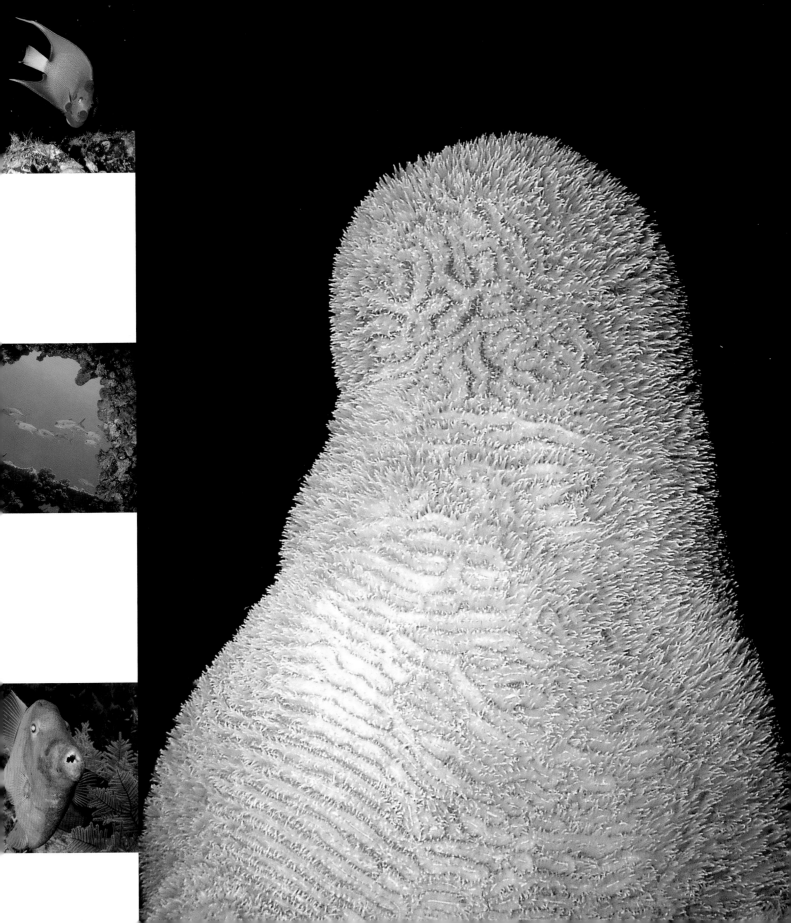

The RMS *Rhone* is considered the finest wreck dive in the Caribbean, and one of the best in the world.

hurricane of 1867, she made a final dash to safety by heading for the open sea before sinking to the ocean floor just a few miles away. Today she is cloaked in corals and sits at a depth between 30–90 ft; you usually tackle the deep bow first, then the shallow stern on your second dive. It is worth casting an eye over a plan of the wreck before diving (you'll find one on board the resort's boat), as this will help you make sense of what is scattered over the seabed. There is much to see, including the honeymoon suite porthole, restored to glinting brass by divers rubbing for good luck.

The wreck has one major intact section, which was the setting of the 1977 film *The Deep*. You can comfortably swim inside, never losing sight of the blue open water. There is plenty of life, though you may have to search for some of it: yellow moray, lobster, barracuda, jack, grunt, soldierfish, spotted drum, queen angelfish, cowfish, octopus and green moray. Also check out the single remaining cannon, the ship's giant wrench set and the solitary anchor. This is a wonderful dive, full of marine life set against the haunting shapes of the ship enhanced by the filtered light of the sun, and you never know what you might come across in the endless recesses.

ABOVE
Spread across the ocean floor in three sections, the *Rhone* provides endless opportunities for exploring.

ABOVE
The *Rhone* is not the only wreck dive in the waters of Peter Island. This tugboat wreck is now captained by a turtle, which has taken control of the wheelhouse.

BELOW, LEFT
As one of the earliest steel ships, the *Rhone* provides a solid base for 150 years of marine growth.

BELOW, RIGHT
The clear waters around Peter Island offer an excellent diversity of coral life.

It all seems faintly surreal. Sitting in a hot tub on the stern of a 120-ft boat, far from land and in the middle of the warm waters of the Caribbean, you behold all around the spectacle of humpback whales breaching, tail-slapping or just swimming by lazily with their newborn calves. Just a glimpse of such activity would be thrilling witnessed from a cold, rain-lashed, whale-watching boat – here it soon becomes the norm.

BOAT

turks and caicos aggressor II

The *Turks and Caicos Aggressor II* is a 120-ft dive boat. Built in 2003, she normally plies the waters of the Turks and Caicos islands, but for just six weeks a year she steers a few hundred miles off course to the Silver Banks, south of the Dominican Republic. Here you can enjoy the extraordinary experience of getting up close and personal with 40 tonnes of humpback whale. An eight-hour haul from Puerto Plata deposits you midway between the Dominican Republic and the Turks and Caicos islands in the northern Caribbean – it's quite a way, so bring along sea-sickness medication just in case. Once you set anchor, however, you are protected from the ocean swell by an enormous horseshoe reef, so you can put your pills away and relax.

There are berths to suit a range of budgets. The fully air-conditioned cabins come as quads, doubles or a more spacious stateroom. The quads are ideal for families, while the doubles are suitable for couples; note that cabins 8 and 9 are closest to the constantly-running generator. The solitary stateroom is set in the bow and offers a larger bed and a bit more room. Storage space is generally limited, but wetsuits and snorkel gear are all stored on the covered dive deck so there is just enough room to hang your things. Luckily you can definitely pack light as the boat is deeply informal and you're bound not to use all your clothes.

at a glance

Airport	Puerto Plata
Airlines	American Airlines, Continental Airlines
Transfer time	30 mins by car
Cabins	9 (all air-conditioned)
Staff ratio	1
Services	Email, DVD player, jacuzzi, digital cameras for hire, satellite phone
Children	10+
Power type	2-pin flat
Currency	US dollar
GMT	-5
Booking	www.diveinstyle.com

Construction of the boat took two years, overseen by the watchful eye of captain–owner Piers van der Walt, and no detail has been overlooked. Each cabin has a wall-mounted DVD player, and there is an up-to-date selection of over 200 films to choose from. Email accounts are set up on boarding and there's even a satellite phone available, so you're never out of touch – unless, that is, you want to be. Short informative 'whale lectures' and slideshows after dinner help you understand what you are witnessing, but if your attention ever strays, you can just look out the window and see it happening right in front of you.

You spend just five days out on the Silver Banks, with two daily outings on rigid inflatables. After breakfast you're given a thorough briefing from Piers, and then you're off in search of that special encounter. Spending two three-hour sessions on a small rubber boat under the hot sun may sound trying, but as soon as the action starts, any discomfort is swiftly forgotten.

When you leave you are offered a DVD featuring footage shot during your stay. At US$60, it does not come cheap, but it does serve as a wonderful reminder of your adventure; it almost makes you wish you'd left your camera at home and instead focused on enjoying the moment. If you prefer to take your own shots, however, you can choose from an extensive range of digital and 35mm underwater cameras to hire.

The quality of the food varies. Breakfast sets you up for the day with porridge, eggs and pancakes, while lunch is normally some kind of pasta, warmingly welcome after hours either in the water or in a damp wetsuit. Dinner is less satisfying as there is a shortage of fresh ingredients on board; it may be worth asking in advance whether the boat can stock up with mahi mahi at Puerto Plata.

All in all, there is no safer or more comfortable way to experience swimming with humpback whales. After an incredible day in the water with these wonderful creatures, you return to a hot tub, cocktail and movie in bed. It doesn't get much better than this.

Every year, from late January to late March, huge numbers of humpback whales brave the 1,500 mile journey from the north Atlantic to the warm sheltered waters of the Silver Banks, close to the windsurfing mecca of the Dominican Republic. For reasons still unknown to science, they travel here to give birth to their 12-ft calves, mate again, and then turn back for the long haul north. During this 3,000-mile round trip, they never feed.

ABOVE
This could be you, swimming just a few feet away from 40 tonnes of trusting humpback whale.

SNORKELLING

This is a trip where there is no need for the typical 'expect to see' briefing. At the right time of year, the underwater action is guaranteed. You will swim with 40-ft-long, 40-tonne whales and their calves; you will witness their massive breaches and tail slaps; and, if you're lucky, you may even enjoy the company of an inquisitive juvenile or 'Valentine'. These encounters – where you float on the surface and let the whales come to you, and not the other way round – can put you within an arm's length of these magnificent creatures.

Nothing quite prepares you for the first time you slip into the water, mask and snorkel on, and find yourself hovering above a fully mature, sleeping behemoth. Even though you are completely safe, it's impossible to keep your heart from racing; you are torn between fear and wonder. It is quite simply a privilege to be in the water with these amazing mammals, especially when you consider that despite being hunted by man, they are one of the few animals that will allow you to come between them and their newborn offspring.

The best thing is, you need no qualifications to enjoy this incredible experience. If you can snorkel, you can swim literally within inches of some of nature's biggest and greatest stars, and you will come away with memories to last a lifetime. It is truly magical.

at a glance

Level	Easy
Visibility	50–80 ft
Snorkelling	Unbelievable
Wetsuits	3mm
Coral	Poor
Marine life	Humpback whale, spotted dolphin, nudibranchs
Other	Marine park

OPPOSITE TOP
Humpback whales aren't all there is to see. It is quite common to come across schools of dolphin, which seem to enjoy interacting with man in these remote waters.

OPPOSITE MIDDLE
From tail slaps to breaches, you will encounter the whole spectrum of the humpback's vocabulary.

OPPOSITE BOTTOM
The whales are so close you could touch them. Normally the mother remains in deeper water, casting a watchful eye as her calf rises to greet you.

If your vision of this first Caribbean Aman is of beautiful white-sand beaches, perfect water, fabulous food, great service, endless space and original architecture all set in luxuriant palm-studded manicured grounds, you would be spot on except for the grounds. Like the rest of the Caribbean, these islands are not naturally home to palms and the designers have added to the indigenous shrubs and trees rather than importing vegetation.

HOTEL amanyara

The trip from the airport is not that inspiring, but that changes the moment you enter the grounds. On sand roads for the final approach, it is clear that this is one of the prime spots on the islands, as aside from Parrot Cay with its own island, the rest of the high-end resorts are all crowded around the once unspoilt Grace Bay beach, a perfect strand of pure white fine powder. Here on route to Amanyara there is no one else for miles; for now, this is as remote as you could want, and yet is still within an easy hour's drive of a golf course.

The resort is focused around the large tranquil reflecting pool that mirrors the principal buildings dominated by the soaring bar, an out-of-scale structure that somehow works, mainly because of its amazing timber ceiling. Beyond, another signature Aman infinity pool, this time in black quartz, bordered by oversize daybeds, looking out over the rocky coast and perfect turquoise sea. Until now you might have thought you were in the Far East, but at the beach bar you discover the Caribbean, evidenced by the beautiful unspoilt view along the private strand. These islands are renowned for having some of the finest beaches in the world, and this is one of the best. Having said that, this is not a 'toes in the sand' type of resort.

There are two principal room types; both are approached by winding stone paths. There are 17 ocean-front rooms, hidden back in the

at a glance

Airport	Providenciales
Airlines	British Airways, American Airlines
Transfer time	25 mins by 4 x 4
Rooms	17 ocean view, 23 lake view and 20 villas (all air-conditioned)
Staff ratio	2+
Activities	Cinema, swimming pool, deep-sea fishing, tennis, kayaking, hobie cat, spa, golf (45 mins), daily snorkel trips
Services	Wi-fi, television, DVD, free VoIP, iPod docking, room service
Other	Mobile phones allowed
Children	Any age
Power type	2-pin US
Currency	US dollar
GMT	-5
Booking	www.diveinstyle.com

scrub, some opening onto small intimate white-sand coves, while the Pond Villas appear to float on inland man-made seawater lakes.

The spacious rooms are traditional Aman with incredibly comfortable beds, gentle lighting, but not at the cost of dedicated reading lights and more electric blinds than a small boy could wish for. While initially disappointed not to be in a sea-view room, I soon appreciated the peaceful charm of the pond as your bed directly faces out onto your terrace and the water beyond. It is like being on a very still boat.

Internally you cannot fault these cool rooms: terrazzo floors, three walls of glass, lofty honey-coloured timber ceilings, sumptuous down pillows and a typically vast semi-open-plan bathroom. They are both impressive and yet cosy. In short, pretty unbeatable, but then given the price so they should be. And yet this is one of the things about this group: the hotels are expensive but you never come away feeling you have been short changed. They promise and they perform – simple.

Meals are served where you want them. Breakfast on a sala by the pool, lunch in the beach bar, dinner hovering above the infinity pool, or in the calm air-conditioned comfort of the restaurant, the choices are pretty endless. Speaking of food, the Swiss chef, late of Lizard Island in Australia (another resort fabled for its food) delivers the goods again here. A light Eastern touch is apparent throughout the inventive and delicious menu – fusion cooking might be too strong a word for it.

The dinner menu changes every night, and seemingly whatever you choose is exquisite. So in simple terms, if you want better food save the taxi fare – it isn't there. So how would I summarize this first Caribbean venture for the Aman group? While not feeling that 'Caribbean', especially as so many of the staff are Asian, the resort carries it off and in the setting and style it fits the Aman profile perfectly, another sensational Aman resort. Could this be the best resort in the Caribbean?

The immaculate dive center with expansive facilities, oversized showers and endless fluffy towels sits between the beach bar and the beach. A full selection of new BCs and wetsuits look lost in the capacious changing area with private lockers. The center is run and manned by Big Blue, the islands' top dive operator who specializes in small groups and thus provides almost private diving.

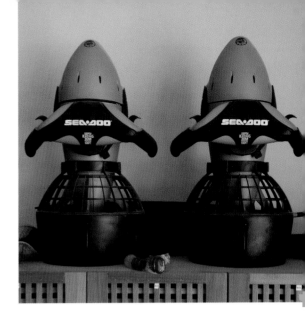

DIVE CENTER

The beach, with its incredible sand and truly translucent waters, some of the clearest in the world, is an invitation to take that first step in your training – it is just a large private pool, albeit that there is no protective reef and thus on occasion can be storm affected. I can think of no better place to learn, especially with the added plus of receiving top-quality instruction from the team. If you are nervous about the whole concept ask for Mark.

Pick-up is directly off the beach on one of Big Blue's catamarans, and with the nearest site just a few minutes away, it could not be easier; the best diving, however, lies further afield and their boats are more than up to the job, being catamarans with their soft ride. Crewed by friendly divers (you could even get Paul who might rearrange your concept of the English) who have known these waters for years: they know the sites intimately and always carry a full range of cold drinks and on day trips the Amanyara will provide you with a delicious lunch basket to complement what should be a memorable day. If you want more adventure, then they are up to the task: just ask, as Mark is always keen to seek out new spots to dive in this still relatively uncharted archipelago. In short, the perfect complement to the Amanyara and the service is a level up from when the resort first opened.

at a glance

Boats	26-ft (open) and 40-ft (covered) catamaran
Group size	4–6
Instructors	8+
Languages	English
Courses	All PADI
Children	12+
Other	Computer hire, nitrox, gear prep and wash down, drinks, lunches, private guides available
Website	www.bigblue.tc

ABOVE
This is all about wall diving and endless visibility.

Diving in these islands is all about walls, plunging walls from 60 ft down to 6,000 ft and beyond, a vertical abyss over which you hover, never sure of what might be out there in the blue: anything from sharks or eagle rays to dolphins or humpback whales in season. I have heard claims of diving with mantas here, but if that is what you are looking for then I suggest you go to Indonesia or Yap.

RIGHT
Flamingo tongue shells hang like baubles from fans.

ABOVE
Octopus are plentiful but inevitably difficult to see with their incredible adaptive camouflage.

RIGHT
A nervous butterflyfish peaks out from among the coral.

DIVING

at a glance

Local sites	10+
Level	Easy to moderate
Visibility	75–150 ft
Must-dives	Black Coral Forest and the Crack (local) Sandbore Channel and French Cay
Snorkelling	Daily 1-hour trip to nearby reefs – better slightly further afield
Wetsuits	3mm all year round
Coral	Healthy hard corals, including black coral
Marine life	Humpback whale, great barracuda, reef shark, great hammerhead shark, dolphin, eagle ray
Other	Hyperbaric chamber on Providenciales. Most diving in Marine Parks

Amanyara is situated on what was once one of the great wall dives of the islands, however, time has moved on and now only really Amphitheatre and Black Coral Forest merit a dive; for the non-claustrophobic, Hole in the Wall can be interesting. These dives are fine because they are easily accessible and gentle and big life can, and does, turn up at any time. The real fun, however, lies further afield and you should spend as little time as necessary on the house reef and make tracks elsewhere.

French Cay and Sandbore Channel are the two must-dives, the former being a day trip, the latter easily accessible from the resort but weather and tide dependent. The neighbouring island of West Caicos can also offer good diving, especially Anchor, named after an 18th-century anchor lodged in the reef and now encrusted with coral. That aside, though, the development of this once remote island seems to have negatively impacted on the marine life.

French Cay is a wonderful 45-minute run across the virgin shallows to the drop-off on the southern side of the islands and on a good day is worth the trip in itself. Out of sight of land, your boat cleaves the transparent water above dolphin, rays and shark, all silhouetted against the sand shallows mere feet deep and for miles in every

ABOVE
Resident green turtles are normally very approachable.

RIGHT
Groupers of many species abound, but wary of humans and their dinner habits, they are tricky to approach.

RIGHT
Diving here you never know what large life might turn up: humpback whales, eagle ray, shark or, in this case, make do with dolphin.

direction. On arrival you will find a very healthy reef with beautiful
vertical walls clad in gorgonians with all manner of life, specifically
grazing turtles and guaranteed shark sightings: inquisitive sightings.
Eagle rays, often in groups, even humpback whales in season can
be frequent visitors and if you are lucky and more likely if you are
in a small group, you might just encounter the aptly named *giant*
hammerhead who calls French Cay home. I saw it and it set my heart
racing with his huge dorsal fin and clear interest in making a new
friend. Not unsurprisingly, I fluffed the photo opportunity.

In short, the further from the hub of 'Provo' you get, the further from
man, the healthier the marine environment becomes. The two sites
at French Cay, Double D and G spot, are uncrowded and the water,
assuming the tide is right, is very clear. It can get a little bumpy in
winter, but if this is the case, then the team will take you five minutes
to shelter in the lee of the tiny protected and deserted cay, perfect for
lunch. One point to note is that given the depth of the reef wall over
here, it is well worth diving nitrox to add to your bottom time as there
is much to see and endless coral heads to explore. The better your air
consumption as your fellow divers ascend, the better your chance of
the bigger sightings.

With the exception of the ABC islands (Aruba, Bonaire and
Curaçao) in the far south or off the coast of Belize, Caribbean
diving is not renowned for its quality, probably because of man's
relentless pressure on the area. Having dived in the Turks and
Caicos islands over the past 20 years, the change is clear and
in this instance it has not been especially helped by wanton
development with little in the way of genuine governmental
concern for the marine environment. However, this is classic
wall diving and there still remains a good chance of seeing some
big life. Having the Amanyara as your home base just makes
the package all that much sweeter.

Just to the south of Corsica in the western Mediterranean, the Italian island of Sardinia is a mountainous slab of granite blessed with endless white-sand coves, and offers some of the best diving in the Mediterranean. In 1960 the Aga Khan led a group of investors in buying some 35 miles of its most stunning coastline, and proceeded to transform it into what is now known as the Costa Smeralda or the Emerald Coast, named after the distinctive colour of the island's surrounding waters.

To many, the Costa Smeralda is Sardinia. Much of its appeal today is thanks to its developers' foresight in imposing strict controls on building and careful protection of the natural environment. Thus, even after over 40 years of development, the place still seems relatively unspoilt, and new restrictions on building on the coast mean it's likely to stay that way.

Sardinia is quiet for most of the year, but things heat up in July and August, when the sun shines at its brightest and the beautiful people arrive in droves. For a six-week period, luxury yachts moor in the bays while their owners relax in the picturesque town of Porto Cervo and party at the appropriately named Billionaire's Club. Prices rocket due to the incredible demand, and many resorts stay open for just four months. Still, the reason people keep coming here is the promise of tranquillity, and Hotel Pitrizza gives you just that.

HOTEL PITRIZZA

Tucked behind its own private beach on a small granite headland, Pitrizza occupies a prime position on Sardinia's wild but exclusive shoreline. First opened in 1963 and substantially refurbished in 1990, its design is in keeping with the rest of the Costa Smeralda: nature has been respected, and the grounds and architecture are in perfect harmony with the rugged landscape of Sardinia's northeastern coast.

sardinia

HOTEL pitrizza

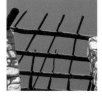

The rustic stone buildings blend into the background so well that they are reminiscent of hobbit-dwellings, albeit incredibly stylish ones. Understated in design, the Pitrizza's rooms feature white-plastered walls accented by local tiles and furniture. A panoramic sheet of glass separates your bedroom from the terrace. Many of the rooms overlook the Med; if you want the very best, go for a room west of the main clubhouse. Even more upscale are the hotel's 15 suites. And then there is always a white-washed villa with its own tiny private beach, or else up on the Capa di Sopra are two hilltop villas with private pools.

At the heart of the hotel is a bar and an indoor–outdoor dining area with views to the beach. Dining tends to be alfresco, looking out over the signature saltwater infinity pool hewn out of granite. Food is included in the hotel rate for a relatively modest supplement.

Pitrizza is only open from May to September; the water is too cold to swim in at any other time of year. As the temperature soars, so do hotel rates all over the Costa Smeralda – but you'll be staying in what is by all accounts the finest hotel in the Mediterranean, which also happens to have access to some of the region's best and most varied diving. In Europe, diving in style doesn't get much better than this.

at a glance

Airport	Olbia
Airlines	Easyjet, Meridiana
Transfer time	30 mins by taxi
Rooms	56 villas (all air-conditioned)
Staff ratio	2+
Activities	Watersports, golf, tennis, squash, horse-riding, fishing, go-karting, spa, swimming pool, gym
Services	Internet, telephone, television, DVD player, room service
Other	Mobile phones
Children	All ages
Power type	2-pin round
Currency	Euro
GMT	+1
Booking	www.diveinstyle.com

Proteus Diving is an easy five-minute drive from Hotel Pitrizza, and a private charter will pick you up from the hotel's beach if you request it. You generally have to look after your own gear so it's easiest to rent theirs, but this isn't a problem; you get excellent and personalized service from the small, friendly team. Most importantly, you will only ever dive with five in your group (some local centers lead dives that number in the twenties).

DIVE CENTER

The boat is a 20-ft Zodiac with a powerful outboard and is excellent for travelling to the sites, most of which are reached within 30 minutes over the protected and usually calm waters. There are 15 other dive operators on the Costa Smeralda so the sea may look a bit too busy for comfort, but don't worry – there are about 40 dive sites, so underwater crowds are never an issue.

Like the hotel, the diving season is dependent on the weather and lasts from May to September. The water can be chilly early on but reaches a relatively balmy 25°C (roughly 75°F) at the peak of summer; June is a good month to come, but September is possibly the best as the sea is still warm but the crowds will have disappeared. The center has wetsuits for all conditions (offering double 5mm protection in May), but as always it's best to bring your own mask and, in this instance, a hooded vest. Combine this with their equipment, and even the colder months shouldn't be an issue.

Dives take place either in the morning or the afternoon. It's all very civilized and personal, with no jarringly early starts and normally just one dive per trip. Private charters offer the most flexibility and you can even take a two-tank dive, enjoying your surface interval with lunch on one of the small white-sand beaches on the coastline.

at a glance

Boats	20-ft Zodiac (wet, open)
Group size	5
Instructors	2
Languages	English, Italian, Spanish
Courses	All PADI, CMAS
Children	14+
Other	Computer hire, food and drinks, private charters, nitrox, rebreathers
Website	www.proteusdiving.it

Diving the dramatic canyons and
passages of this coastline is an
almost architectural experience.

Diving in Sardinia offers aquarium-like
conditions with almost limitless visibility.
Often described as the most exciting diving in the
Mediterranean, it is both varied and suitable for
all divers, from novices to the more experienced.

DIVING

A major reason why the diving is so good is that this corner of
Sardinia is actually a national park, La Maddelena. You'll come
across more fish life here than anywhere else in the Med; at Picchi
di Punta Coticcio, for instance, there are moray, octopus, large
grouper, beautiful nudibranchs, scorpionfish, lobster and schools
of castagnole, creating a scene reminiscent of the Red Sea. There
is not much big life at any of the sites, but you can find a large group
of good-sized groupers to the north in the islands of Lavezzi, which
seem totally unfazed by divers' paparazzi-like behaviour.

The most spectacular aspect of the diving is the underwater
landscape. Sardinia's islands are made of granite, with rock
formations reminiscent of the Seychelles sliding into the depths.
Secche dei Monarci, a pair of underwater pinnacles, is renowned
for its vivid red gorgonian corals, while Grotta di San Francesco is
an experience in itself: after being greeted by a grouper known as
the Receptionist, you enter a tunnel to emerge in a clear aquamarine
pool, open to the skies and framed by overhanging rock. Soaring
granite walls, canyons, gulleys, caves and current-swept peaks
provide a stunning backdrop for any dive, and the remarkable range
of sea life in this so-called dead sea is just the icing on the cake.

at a glance

Local sites	15
Level	Easy to advanced
Visibility	100 ft
Must-dives	Punta del Papa, Lavezzi
Snorkelling	None
Wetsuits	5mm+
Coral	None
Marine life	Grouper, Mediterranean moray, octopus, scorpionfish, conger eel, nudibranchs, schools of barracuda, electric ray, red gorgonians
Other	Day trips, night dives, marine park

This is probably the only
place in Italy where you can
see calamari not on a plate;
large groupers have made
a comeback in this marine
park and are relatively
approachable, especially
at Lavezzi; moray eels and
conger eels inhabit the
craggy walls; surprisingly
beautiful scorpionfish
swim in these waters, their
perfectly camouflaged
colours revealed only
by the camera's flash.

Egypt's Sinai Peninsula is a triangular wedge of raw shimmering desert jutting down into the Red Sea and like many deserts is topographically stunning. But here the contrast of red sand running into clear blue water is especially striking. Almost at the tip of this arrowhead lies Sharm el-Sheikh, perfectly placed to access the world-renowned dive sites of Ras Mohammed National Park and the Straits of Tiran.

Once a sleepy fishing village, Sharm used to be the only settlement on this desolate yet dramatic stretch of the Red Sea, and as recently as 1982 there was only one place to stay. Things have moved on in recent years, and while the town is still backed by arid hills and *wadis* rolling out of the desert, today it hosts some 138 hotels either completed or under construction. Most of them cater to tourists on cheaper package holidays, but this shouldn't have any impact on your stay. Just head straight to the Four Seasons – of all the hotels, this oasis of a resort stands head and shoulders above the rest.

The only land bridge between the two continents of Africa and Asia, Sinai borders Israel to the north and faces Saudi Arabia across the Gulf of Aqaba to the east. While the peninsula's strategic significance has made it synonymous with a troubled past, visitors should not be put off coming here. If there are risks, then they are unlikely to be greater than those of modern living anywhere in the world, especially once cosseted within the resort.

A few years ago the site of the Four Seasons was simply desert – breathtaking and dramatic, but nonetheless just sand and rock. Now, thanks to the miracles of desalination, it has been transformed into a verdant oasis. Opened in 2002, the resort's grounds tumble down a gentle incline to the shores of the Red Sea, some 300 mature palms marking the stark boundary between the hotel's lush gardens and the arid surrounding landscape.

HOTEL four seasons sharm el-sheikh

This is still the best resort here. A broad drive leads you to the hub of the hotel, a spacious structure clad in cream stone and defined by Egyptian architectural detailing. Here you will find the reception and a number of restaurants, which look out over the grounds to the water below. To the north of this are the 64 two-bedroom suites, ideal for families, while to the south lie the other 136 guest rooms.

Despite offering more than 200 rooms, this is not a place that crowds you. The lush gardens are broken up by small, bougainvillea-strewn piazzas on different levels, reached by either wide stone paths or an electric tram (a child's delight). These unique spaces lend the resort the feel of a small village. You rarely see the complex as a whole; instead, you are continually moving from one beautifully landscaped area to another.

All the newly refurbished rooms have private terraces, some of which give directly onto the gardens or, for a premium, offer lofty views of the land falling away to the sea below. The marble-floored interiors are simple yet elegant, and at the end of the day provide a cool, quiet haven, complete with incredibly comfortable bed – a Four Seasons trademark – fluffy pillows, delicious duvet and (naturally) Egyptian cotton sheets, changed daily. The bathrooms are just as luxurious.

at a glance

Airport	Sharm el-Sheikh direct or via Cairo
Airlines	British Airways, Egypt Air, Monarch
Transfer time	10 mins by limousine
Rooms	210 (all air-conditioned)
Staff ratio	4
Activities	St Catherine's Monastery, Bedouin camp, desert quad biking and horseriding, coloured canyon trip, swimming pools, spa, gym, yoga, croquet, planned golf course
Services	Telephone, television, internet, DVD and CD player, iPod, room service
Other	Mobile phones
Children	All ages
Power type	2-pin round
Currency	Egyptian pound, US dollar
GMT	+2
Booking	www.diveinstyle.com

To get back my youth I would do anyting in the world except take exercise get up early or be respectable

The architects did a superb job, but it is the landscapers who have really triumphed. They have planted no fewer than 1,800 palms, and in a land where water is at a premium, no courtyard is short of a trickling fountain. A stream flows down a series of rock-strewn beds from the heart of the hotel, and the soothing sound of moving water blends intoxicatingly with the scent of jasmine and the colours of the vegetation.

The selection of restaurants is seemingly endless with no less than seven possibilities. The Reef Grill, perched on a small bluff above the sand, offers fabulous views of the island of Tiran and is perfect for a simple lunch or light dinner. Up at the hotel itself, you can dine at the Moroccan–Lebanese restaurant Arabesque, Il Frantoio for Italian, or feast on sushi in the Observatory Lounge. The food is excellent, if on the expensive side, so you may want to load up on the delicious and extensive breakfast, included in the room rate.

Although none of the hotels on Sinai's coastline has a world-class beach, the Four Seasons has made the most of its own red-sand crescent with an array of carefully positioned private niches, which give the impression of seclusion even when the beach is full. You can swim directly off the shore, but it's best to grab your mask and fins and walk to the end of a jetty, where you can drop into some 15 ft of water and snorkel with lionfish.

The staff are truly exceptional: welcoming, friendly and keen to help in whatever way they can. They do a first-class job at looking after children, but if you'd rather avoid the kids, steer clear of the resort at the end of October when many schools are on holiday.

If you want a change from diving or snorkelling, there is plenty to keep you busy. Facing the water, it is easy to forget the beauty of the desert behind you, where you can do everything from quad-biking to paying homage to St Catherine's Monastery at the base of Mount Sinai.

The Four Seasons is not a small hotel, but feels much smaller than it is. If you're after truly guaranteed sunshine, wonderful diving, superb friendly service and a luxurious, impeccably managed resort with local flavour, look no further.

Sinai Blues is located at the core of the Four Seasons' beach, not more than five minutes from any of the rooms. This highly professional operation offers both dive trips and snorkelling excursions, and a truly extensive range of Scubapro gear is available to hire. There are never more than six divers to an instructor, so you can count on enjoying individual attention both on the boat and underwater.

DIVE CENTER

The Red Sea is very heavily dived, and the Egyptian government has stepped in to limit the number of dive boats in its waters. Although this is apparently capped at 300, all 300 seem to find their way to Sharm. Don't be surprised by the armada of white hulls crowding the horizon on the way back from your morning dive.

The secret to avoiding all this is to wind your body clock a few hours forward. If you are going south to Ras Mohammed, it's best to leave the dock by 7 a.m.; you won't be back until early afternoon, so order a packed breakfast and lunch basket before you set out. If you are heading north to the Straits of Tiran, then an even earlier start of 6 a.m. is advisable; once you've enjoyed some solitary diving, the fast RIB will return you to the hotel in time for the amazing breakfast.

Sinai Blues' fleet is managed by the delightful Riham. A high-speed rigid inflatable will take you to the Straits in under 15 minutes, while a larger motorboat will transport you to the more distant sites of Ras Mohammed. The crew more than live up to the Egyptian reputation for hospitality, looking after your gear, rinsing it for you, and helping you in and out of the water. Despite heavy demand at peak times, the dive center never loses its personal touch, and with 12 instructors to hand, this is a great place to learn to dive.

at a glance

Boats	28 ft+ (wet open, dry covered)
Group size	6
Instructors	12
Languages	English, Arabic, French, Flemish, Russian, Swedish, Danish, Portuguese, German, Italian, Japanese, Spanish
Courses	All PADI
Children	8–10 for Bubblemaker course, 10+ for open-water certificate
Other	Computer hire, nitrox on request, food and drinks if ordered in advance, private charters, gear prep and wash down, marine biologist
Website	www.sinaiblues.com

The Red Sea has some wonderful diving, and despite its popularity, Sharm el-Sheikh still offers some of the best. This is mainly thanks to its location, right at the point where the Red Sea splits into the Gulfs of Suez and Aqaba. In addition, there is a plethora of diveable wrecks along Egypt's coastline.

DIVING

Some argue that the ultimate diving in the Red Sea is only to be found on a live-aboard ploughing its way either to the Brother Islands or to Sudan and the far south. However, around Sharm you can find examples of virtually every known coral species in this body of water, together with nearly as many fish species as there are on Australia's Great Barrier Reef.

Most of the diving is done at two locations: the Straits of Tiran just to the north, and the Ras Mohammed National Park to the south. Ras Mohammed is the place most people have heard about, but don't forget Tiran, which is just as rewarding and also happens to be more conveniently located. There are well over 35 immediate sites to choose from, so you could easily spend a week here without diving the same spot twice.

The topography of the reefs varies from gentle slopes to full walls. The one thing they all have in common is that the top is always just a few feet beneath the surface, ensuring that not a second of your time underwater is wasted; your safety stop is as good as the rest of the dive. This also means the reefs are fantastic for snorkellers, who can even join the dive trips to Ras Mohammed. Closer to home, the hotel beach rewards snorkellers with schools of lionfish and

at a glance

Local sites	36
Level	Easy to advanced
Visibility	100 ft+
Must-dives	Small Crack, Shark Reef, Yolanda Reef, Jackson Reef
Snorkelling	Very good on house reef, excellent from dive boat
Wetsuits	7mm December–April, 5mm May–June, 3mm July–September, 5mm October–November
Coral	Excellent
Marine life	Schooling hammerhead, jack and barracuda, silky, grey reef, leopard and whale shark, Napoleon wrasse, crocodilefish, bottlenose dolphin, manta and eagle ray, giant moray
Other	Day trips, night dives, wreck dives, marine park, hyperbaric chamber in Sharm el-Sheikh

ABOVE
A member of the sea urchin family, devoid of its normal array of spines, is easy prey for triggerfish and pufferfish.

OPPOSITE, TOP
Red Sea bannerfish are often found in pairs or larger schools.

OPPOSITE, MIDDLE
Night dives are the only time you will ever find a stationary parrotfish. For once, you can appreciate their beautiful colourings at your leisure.

OPPOSITE, BOTTOM
Geometric morays are one of three types frequently found in the Red Sea. Giant morays can easily measure over 9 ft long.

OPPOSITE, MAIN PICTURE
Relaxed hawksbill turtles are a common sight, especially in the Straits of Tiran.

OPPOSITE

With up to 150-ft visibility, the
Red Sea's pristine reefs are
home to well over a thousand
species of fish and over 200
types of coral. It is not just
the breadth of marine life,
from tiny glassfish to giant
whale shark, but also the
sheer quantity that makes
this such a great area to dive.

RIGHT, FROM TOP
TO BOTTOM

There is literally a blizzard of
life on most of the Red Sea's
reefs. Despite over-diving,
it is both plentiful and in
excellent health; stunning
nudibranchs (literally nude gills),
the wavy bits on the back, are
a common sight; the drop-offs
at Ras Mohammed are stuffed
with life.

even a resident crocodilefish, while those who want to learn to dive
can do no better than here, there being no real current to speak of.

Both hard and soft corals abound and are in excellent health.
An amazing diversity of sea life inhabits them, ranging from the
distinctive technicolour anthias to schools of hammerhead, jack and
barracuda, in the summer months. Giant green moray are present
on every dive, and they live up to their name: it's not unheard of
to find a relaxed 9-ft eel fully exposed on the coral, some with truly
vast heads.

One of Sharm's most outstanding dives and snorkels is at
Small Crack, right at the tip of the Sinai Peninsula. In the right
conditions, you start out on the outer edge of the reef where there
is a chance to see leopard shark and schools of barracuda and jack.
Within Small Crack itself, the variety of life is spectacular, and since
it's very shallow there is no need for a torch as all the colours are
incredibly vivid. It's the nearest thing to a flooded florists.

The Red Sea has a number of wreck dives. The *Thistlegorm* is the
most famous and requires an early start as it is quite distant and
often crowded. You'll love it if your fantasy happens to be sitting
astride a sunken 1940 BSA motorbike or swimming among Bren-
gun carriers, though otherwise you may find it disappointing as
the sea life here is nothing special.

There are simply too many sites to describe, let alone recommend,
as they each have their day; what you will see is really a matter of
luck, the season and your instructor's knowledge. If you can bear
the heat, the best time to dive the Red Sea is probably midsummer,
as this brings schooling fish and shark. Nonetheless, whenever you
visit, be sure to get an early start and you will be richly rewarded.

Oman, or to give it its full and rather more romantic title, The Sultanate of Oman, is something of a bizarre cartographer's anomaly. Indeed, this is the only country I can think of which has been voluntarily split into two distinct parts. Cleanly divided by the United Arab Emirates, most remarkably for the Middle East, this anomaly was not created by an anonymous civil servant somewhere deep in the Foreign Office armed with ruler and quill pen. The Musandam Peninsula, as this northern territory is now known, is in effect the northern exclave of Oman and guards the southern approaches of the vital Straits of Hormuz.

Oman is primarily an arid desert with mountains to the north and south, an extenuated coastline to the Arabian Sea, with a small, young population of just 3.5 million, mostly hugging the coastline. Independent since 1650, in the late 18th century the newly established Sultanate signed the first of its friendship treaties with the UK. Under the guidance of the Sultan, Qaboos bin Said al-Said, the country is an effective monarchy which he has endeavoured to open up to the outside world and with a moderate independent foreign policy has sought and maintained good relations with all Middle East countries. With over 2,000 km of virtually empty beaches, this formerly totally oil-dependent state is seeking to expand its economy away from this dwindling resource; however, nature has not been entirely un-generous and the country retains substantial gas deposits. Tourism remains a relatively infant industry and is part of the charm of the country, no better evidenced than in the far north, home to Zighy Bay.

Tucked up in the top of what is effectively Oman part 2, this resort boasts an innovative means of arrival, your first sight of your new temporary home possibly being from about 1,000 ft. Strapped to Itsu, the local paragliding champion, you float serenely down to the perfect white-sand beach of this desolate bay. It may be a wrench from the immaculate 4 x 4 that has cosseted you during the two-hour ride from Dubai, but I strongly suggest you find the energy as not only is it the most novel way to check in anywhere, but also the best.

zighy bay

HOTEL **zighy bay**

From ground level the immediate impression is less than inspiring. The arid Hajar mountains that bookend this bay surround a parched landscape. The resort entrance is through a small souk and then the unimposing beige plastered walls of the reception or 'Sablah' greet you. The design is based on a stone Berber village set around an oasis (palms, pool and gurgling spring), and at first glance even this is not exactly breathtaking even though it has been beautifully executed. A golf cart hisses you almost silently along hot sand paths to your room and, if your budget permits, I strongly suggest you make it one on the front row opening directly onto the beach. However, every room, most of which are individual in shape and accommodation has its own charm, and more importantly its own pool – this place gets hot. You are greeted by cool bare stone floors, local rugs and the Six Senses routine of a bare backdrop brought to life with splashes of colour and their astonishing attention to detail starting with their now famous pillow menu. All the rooms are incredibly generous and most have a vast bath, indoor and outdoor showers, and the private 'gardens' with terrace, small pool and shaded banquette sitting area.

So what starts out as not looking especially attractive at first glance slowly begins to morph. You literally get unwrapped by the Six Senses format of 'slow life' and shed your tension and concerns. Whether it is the ever

at a glance

Airport	Dubai
Airlines	Emirates, British Airways, Qatar, South African Airways, Singapore Airlines, Air France and most major airlines
Transfer time	90 mins by 4 x 4 (paraglider or speedboat option for last leg but pre-book)
Rooms	79 and 3 villas (all with private pools and air-conditioned)
Staff ratio	2
Activities	Paragliding, desert adventures, hiking, water skiing, wakeboarding, wind surfer, knee board, tubing
Services	Full spa, DVD and CD, television, telephone, gym, private 'butler' service, private pools, main swimming pool, room service, wi-fi
Children	All ages, babysitters available
Power type	3-pin UK
Currency	US dollar, Omani rial
GMT	+4 (Zighy time is 1 hour ahead of Dubai)
Booking	www.diveinstyle.com

friendly smiling staff, the unbelievable food, the sensational spa, the endless sun or just the relaxed pace (no one ever seems in a hurry and yet everything just seems to happen), 'slow life' takes over. The wide crescent beach offers excellent swimming, although flip-flops or similar are somewhat of a must given there can be a little tar, a by-product of tankers flushing their tanks on their way out of the Gulf. But these will be just about the only shoes you will need during your stay.

As for the food, here Zighy Bay excels, not only in the quality and variety, but also in the choice of locations. The choice is yours at the main restaurant, whether inside or outside overlooking the pool and the sea, set up high to get the best of the wind. In the hotter months, the air-conditioned alternative would be a must. Every day there is a themed menu, whether Arabian BBQ, Italian or Indian and it is all perfectly prepared. However, the real highlight, literally, is 'The Edge'. Three times a week you can 'eat out' 1,000 ft up the towering cliffs in what has to be one of the most fantastic dining experiences anywhere. Perched outside on 'the edge', the very location would give health and safety a fit, I can think of nowhere better. Ideally, this should be prefaced by a glass of champagne with canapés taken on a pillowed sofa higher up the hill on the edge of the drop, but at £30 a glass, it will probably just be the one (huge taxes and convoluted distribution channels account for outrageous prices for alcohol).

To summarize, this is a resort that really grows on you, a pampering escape, and coupled with the excellent diving makes for a fantastic holiday, although, great as it is, a week would probably be enough.

There is little I can report on the center primarily because when I visited it was only just fresh off the drawing board. However, by the time you read this I will have been able to post a report on www.diveinstyle.com. I had to bring this exceptional resort to your attention because knowing how the Six Senses operate, from years of experience, I am more than confident the dive center and service will live up to the promise.

DIVE CENTER

I dived with the local team, some of the nicest divemasters you will find, nothing was too much trouble and I had to do absolutely nothing. The plan is for a new dive center and restaurant down at the effectively private marina, an easy five-minute ride from the hotel to the end of the bay. As they propose to take the diving in house in late 2009, and mirror the Soneva Fushi dive model (part of the Six Senses group) they have the perfect benchmark to borrow from and the arrival of the Luxury Dow *Zighy Al Aqua* seems to indicate they are already well on the way.

We can report that at present you are ferried by a fast and comfortable 27-ft speedboat along the arid but dramatic coastline and the chances are you will see nothing more than the occasional fishing boat. An excellent pre-ordered Zighy picnic lunch accompanies you, but given that most of the dive sites benefit from morning sun, I am afraid an early departure is mandatory. The pace is, however, very relaxed and the early lunchtime break is normally taken in the shade of the dramatic cliffs with not another boat for miles.

Here, for sure, you will be diving alone, and that today is a rare privilege, a great contrast between Oman and the Red Sea.

at a glance

Boats	50-ft Luxury Dow (dry, covered) and 27-ft speed boat+ (dry and covered)
Group size	4+
Instructors	1
Languages	English
Courses	PADI
Children	12+
Other	Excellent Zighy picnic lunches

The Musandam Peninsula is known as the 'Norway of Arabia' with 'fiords' and dramatic pink-skinned cliffs dropping vertically into the sea. There are no barrier reefs here. Instead you dive mostly under the towering cliffs that plunge almost vertically into the depths. It's not far from being a genuine alternative to the Red Sea but without the crowds.

DIVING

All diving is done in the morning so that the east-facing slopes are bathed in sunlight both above and beneath the water. If you are offered afternoon diving, check where they are planning on taking you as direct sunlight on the reef makes such a difference. And beneath the water it is a veritable riot of life set to the soundtrack of the incessant crackle of feeding fish, not unlike being in a bowl of rice krispies. The underwater landscape is principally a boulder field fallen from above, now colonized by both soft and hard corals that somehow seem to thrive in these waters that can heat up to 32°C (90°F) and more. Scientists please explain (actually they are trying to at the moment).

While some sites have their resident specialities, Octopus Rock its seahorses, Ras Sanut or Wonderwall its mantis shrimp, what is fantastic about the diving here is the sheer intensity of life. Triggerfish by the thousand provide the backdrop, huge parrotfish, endless nudibranchs, lionfish and at least five different species of moray eels, honeycomb and the vivid yellow mouth being the most exotic.

Lima South is a wonderful, quite fast drift dive across fields of purple soft corals and, while I missed it by 24 hours, the next day at this site lucky guests had an encounter with a whale shark. Generally, visibility is not that great, but then that explains the riot

at a glance

Local sites	11+
Level	Easy to moderate
Visibility	50 ft+
Must-dives	Limah (North and South), Octopus Rock
Snorkelling	Good
Wetsuits	3mm summer, 5mm+ winter
Coral	Good
Marine life	Whale shark, seahorse, mola mola, mantis shrimp, leopard shark, manta ray, white- and black-tip reef shark

OVE
nudibranchs testify to the
lthy diversity of these reefs.

LOW
ry species here just seems
ger, maybe because man has
ved away.

GHT, ABOVE AND BELOW
autious honeycomb moray;
e site is home to a family of
ge and easily found seahorse
emember they have no eyelids
consider how you would feel
h constant flash!

LOW
tunningly decorated
dibranch.

OPPOSITE, CLOCKWISE
FROM TOP LEFT
Not your traditional reef,
more a colonized rubble field;
a fat multi-hued lobster; no
shortage of life, indeed there
is a constant background
noise, the 'crunch' of coral
feeding fish; large stingrays
are common.

TOP
The colourful and immensely
powerful mantis shrimp out
of his home for a change.

MIDDLE
A yellow-mouthed moray and
trusting cleaner wrasse.

BOTTOM
Green turtle are plentiful.

of life and the presence of whale shark: there have even been fairly
regular encounters with the giant mola mola or sunfish; a thrill
difficult to find. Furthermore, with the advent of the new dive set
up, there is also the chance that in the future more adventurous trips
might be included along this unexplored northern coastline.

What really sets this diving apart from the Red Sea is that no one else
is in the water within miles – you are out here alone and again that
just adds so much to the experience. Given the choice of the now
overcrowded northern Red Sea or the Musandam peninsula, while
the Red Sea definitely offers more variety and colourful reefs, this is
a totally overlooked corner of effectively private diving nirvana; also
with guaranteed sunshine.

Tanzania was born when the republics of Tanganyika and Zanzibar came together in 1964. Home to Mount Kilimanjaro, Africa's highest mountain, this east African nation is the site of one of the world's largest migrations of wild animals, including wildebeest, zebras and gazelles. Though today it is economically poor, its past is incredibly rich, and the most fascinating of its history belongs to Zanzibar.

Once the capital of Oman, one of the wealthiest nations in Africa, Zanzibar has long been known as the Spice Island. Its past is littered with slave traders and colonists, and even now it is a byword for the exotic. The city of Stone Town is definitely worth a visit; the chances are you will pass through here if you're heading to any of the nearby islands. The place to stay is the Serena Inn, right on the beach. It's the perfect base for wandering the city's streets and markets, and provided your room fronts the ocean, you can watch the dhows return from sea against the setting sun. Dinner on the roof of the Emerson and Green Hotel is also a must, but be sure to book in advance.

Just to the north of Zanzibar is the lush, verdant island of Pemba, home to a huge variety of tropical fruits and herbs, as well as endless clove plantations – the air is saturated with their sweet, spicy scent. Hidden away on the coast is Fundu Lagoon. There is no road access so the only way to get here is by private boat, but once you step onto dry land it's like being in a different world – one nestled on an expanse of white powder.

Hidden away on the west coast of Pemba Island, this hotel was carved out of the jungle by a group led by enterprising British fashion designer Ellis Flyte. In 2001 they stumbled on the location almost by mistake, and they then took a gamble on an unknown South African architect for the design. The risk has paid off: the result is a truly unique resort, now finally complete with the recent addition of a stunning double infinity pool.

pemba

HOTEL fundu lagoon

It took just 12 months to transform this place from virgin forest into fully functioning hotel. The construction was no doubt sped up by the owners' hands-on approach: they monitored every step, and even today they spend over half the year running and fine-tuning their creation. Virtually everything is locally built using materials native to the area. This is not the polished, detailed handiwork you would see on the roof of a Fijian buré, but the roughly finished craft you might expect on a safari stay in a Tanzanian village.

Don't be fooled by rustic appearances: you'll find all the creature comforts you need. But what makes this place special is that you never forget where you are. It is all incredibly laid-back and informal, with a strong vein of Africa running throughout: African head carvings, masks and other original items collected on the owners' travels. If this weren't enough to remind you of your location, the families of friendly monkeys and nocturnal bushbabies will do the job for you – just remember not to leave your sunglasses out overnight as they may not be there in the morning!

A long, handcrafted jetty stretches out into the lagoon, branching off to an overwater bar; you'll need to travel its length to access the deeper water, a better place for swimming than the beach.

at a glance

Airport	Zanzibar via Dar es Salaam, Nairobi or Johannesburg
Airlines	British Airways, Emirates, KLM, South African Airways
Transfer time	45 mins by taxi then 20 mins by boat
Rooms	18 (6 with pools)
Staff ratio	3+
Activities	Canoeing, nature walks, forest trips, catamaran charters, dhow cruises, dhow fishing, yoga platform, limited spa, pool table, water skiing, wakeboarding, swimming pool, dolphin safari, humpback whale watching
Services	Television in activities room
Other	Mobile phones
Children	12+
Power type	3-pin square
Currency	Tanzanian shilling, US dollar
GMT	+3
Booking	www.diveinstyle.com

A fine powder-sand path leads to the beachside rooms; an irregular stairway to the hillside ones. The latter offer extra privacy and wonderful views and, open to the trade winds, help keep you cool – a bonus if the ceiling fans aren't enough for you. Every room is essentially a tent – a large, airy African tent, recently upgraded, and swathed in mosquito netting, set on a raised wooden platform and sheltered by a soaring traditional thatched roof. The bed faces directly out over the fabulous view, and the canvas panels fold back to give access to the spacious south-facing timber deck.

Aside from diving, or in season whale watching, chilling out is the order of the day, and that now becomes a serious option next to the new double infinity pool, perched up on the hillside – this radically changes Fundu as beach swimming is not great. The small spa also offers delicious treatments based on perfumed local apothecary oils.

Still, it's worth summoning up the energy for a day trip: divers and snorkellers alike will be rewarded by a visit to nearby Mesali, a marine sanctuary with amazing snorkelling, a fine white-powder beach and excellent swimming in the clear turquoise waters. Or you can take out a 30-ft catamaran for a day's sailing and explore the beautiful beaches scattered in the area around Pemba.

Breakfast and dinner are served in the much larger and now more airy main restaurant overlooking the beach, but lunch is now a real decision, the new hillside pool bar competing with the overwater bar. The food is simple but always well prepared, based on local ingredients including freshly caught fish. The service is attentive if a little slow, but then again, people don't come here for the hectic pace of city life.

Most of Fundu's staff are drawn from the small local village; they are incredibly friendly, and everywhere you go you are greeted with 'Jambo' ('Hi' in Swahili). This is one of the few places where a hotel has really been able to do something for the community. It took a bit of work at first to convince the locals that building a hotel would be a good idea, but the village has been rewarded with improved conditions, including better building materials and the foundation of a new school, all courtesy of the hotel.

Fundu is a different kind of resort. Simple yet stylish, it offers real charm and character – and grows on you at an alarming rate. As the owner's quest to perfect her dream continues, including plans for a pool, the allure of this remote, roughly hewn jewel can only intensify.

Just off the jetty of Fundu Lagoon, this incredibly well-run dive center is the focus of all the resort's water-based activities. Whether you want to snorkel, dive or spend a day on a deserted beach, this operation will make your dreams come true. While the center is quite large – there is a school room and freshwater rinse-down tank – the groups are kept small, and it's up to you to set your own pace.

DIVE CENTER

The center offers an excellent range of gear, from new Scubapro regulators to Aqua Lung BCs in all shapes and sizes, though children are not specifically catered for. The system works perfectly: your fins and mask are kept in a bag marked with a name tag. Foolproof.

The yellow-hulled boats are sturdy, fast 20-ft Rigid Raiders, powered by a pair of outboards. They offer no protection from sun or weather and are only really suited to shorter journeys, so for the full-day 'safaris' be sure to bring an extra towel to sit on. However, they do nudge right up to the shoreline, so access to the boat is not difficult.

Depending on the tide, you reach the boat either by a short walk or a longer trek to the end of the jetty. There are always drinks on board, while a full lunch is provided on the day trips; at Mesali you'll eat under the shade of simple thatch, while on the north and south safaris your meal will be served on a deserted white beach.

The diving here is highly personalized and brilliantly organized. There is little for you to do, and at the end of the day all you have to do is dump your equipment on the boat and head straight for that warm shower. The dive team will then transport your gear to the center, where they will rinse and dry it, ready for your next dive.

at a glance

Boats	20-ft Rigid Raiders (wet, open)
Group size	6
Instructors	5
Languages	English, French
Courses	All PADI
Children	14+
Other	Computer hire, food and drinks, gear prep and wash down

What makes this part of Zanzibar so special is the coral, which is both pristine and extremely varied. Reputed to be the best diving in East Africa, the Pemba Channel, and specifically the area around Mesali, has over 320 coral species – more than twice the number of anywhere else in the region. An added plus is that you will find no one else for miles; exploring these virgin reefs in near-solitude adds a wonderful dimension to the experience.

ABOVE
Many species of ray inhabit the waters off Mesali Island, including this large marble ray.

DIVING

Visibility varies, ranging from about 60 ft to over 100 ft, and to get the most out of diving here you really need to dive on an incoming tide. This will offer you the best visibility and the highest chance of encountering the big pelagics that frequent these waters, the newest and most exciting sightings are of the stunning thresher shark. When you book your holiday it's worth checking with the dive center that you will be able to do at least some of your diving in these conditions.

You can opt to go on a day-trip 'safari' north or south of Pemba, with lunch on a deserted white-sand beach; if you venture south to the Wreck, be sure to go via the Emerald Lagoon, which will reward you with turquoise waters, low-lying sandbanks and tranquil dhows. However, most dives are around Mesali, a beautiful white-sand island base a short boat ride from the hotel, and all the sites are no more than five minutes away. Entry is by backward roll, and there is usually time for dive groups to gather on the surface before descending. A common starting point is Apartment, a comfortable, easy dive centered around a coral bommie rising to some 40 ft; the top is just 20 ft below the surface. This is a hive of activity, literally littered with morays, ranging from the giant green moray to the rarer whitemouth. You'll also find their black-cheeked brother, the most aggressive of the otherwise largely docile family.

at a glance

Local sites	12
Level	Easy to advanced
Visibility	60–100 ft+
Must-dives	Mapanduzi
Snorkelling	Excellent from dive boat
Wetsuits	3mm
Coral	Superb
Marine life	Honeycomb, giant green and whitemouth moray, hammerhead shark, thresher shark, devil ray, eagle ray, torpedo ray, humpback whale, Napoleon wrasse, schooling barracuda, schooling unicornfish, giant grouper, bumphead parrotfish, crocodilefish
Other	Day trips, night dives, wreck dive

OPPOSITE
A school of bannerfish, a dramatic contrast against the clear blue waters.

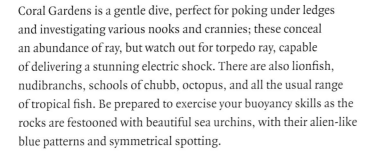

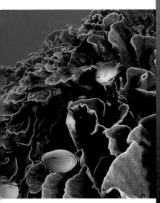

Coral Gardens is a gentle dive, perfect for poking under ledges
and investigating various nooks and crannies; these conceal
an abundance of ray, but watch out for torpedo ray, capable
of delivering a stunning electric shock. There are also lionfish,
nudibranchs, schools of chubb, octopus, and all the usual range
of tropical fish. Be prepared to exercise your buoyancy skills as the
rocks are festooned with beautiful sea urchins, with their alien-like
blue patterns and symmetrical spotting.

If you manage to dive on an incoming tide, Mapanduzi is the main
event. A gentle wall with a deeper drop-off, it goes down to over
100 ft before tumbling into the abyss (which means over 1,000 ft).
You need to descend fast as it only really comes to life when the
strong currents kick in. These can bring in anything from a school
of hammerheads or giant barracuda, to a family of eagle ray or
inquisitive Napoleon wrasse.

Pemba is still relatively uncharted territory, but it has plenty to offer:
marine life of all sizes, acres of coral, an untouched environment,
and some brilliantly organized diving. Now is the time to come.

Mozambique is a nation with a turbulent history. Located at the crossroads between the Middle East and India on the southeastern coast of Africa, it was once a trading port for gold, ivory and slaves. Its fortunes took a turn for the worse in the last century: the former Portuguese colony gained independence in 1975, but was officially one of the poorest nations on earth. A period of socialist mismanagement and 15-year civil war did little to help, with peace finally coming only in 1992.

One of the few positive outcomes of all this is that Mozambique is still relatively untouched – and it is certainly unspoilt by tourism. Yet this beautiful country has plenty to offer visitors: a stunning, completely undeveloped coastline, amazing colonial architecture and some of the friendliest people in Africa.

Foreign investment is on the rise, with more and more resorts opening, mostly low key and sympathetic to their environment. The real pathfinder was Marlin Lodge and it is now joined by the wonderful Vamizi. Both lie just off the Mozambique coast, with Vamizi in the Quirimbas Archipelago to the north and Marlin Lodge in the Bazaruto Archipelago to the south. Separated from one another by a thousand miles, they offer very different tastes of the country, not to mention the diving. But they have one thing in common: both destinations are so untouched that you'll truly have the ocean all to yourself.

mozambique

Let's get the bad news out front: led by the website and the brochure we, and indeed fellow guests, were expecting a sophisticated five-star resort. The reality is different, but none the worse for being so. This is an incredibly comfortable, but otherwise incredibly simple Robinson Crusoe lifestyle, palm-covered huts on a remote and beautiful beach. But to appreciate it fully you need to look at a map and understand just where you are.

vamizi island

HOTEL **vamizi**

To get here, whether you go via Dar where you will probably have to stay overnight (get a transit visa before you go to avoid the scrum on arrival and stay at Oyster Bay if you want a veritable oasis), or via Pemba, you will 'transit' through the war-torn wreckage of an airport that is Mocimboa da Praia. Fifteen minutes later you touch down on the island and after a 30-minute safari-style Land Rover ride, you finally arrive at the hotel.

Vamizi is simple, very simple and feels like a luxury eco resort. There is no swimming pool, no room service, no telephones, no spa, no television, no sop to the modern world. A stunning strip of the softest white powder with lapping turquoise seas, broken by islets of volcanic rock, and set along this strand are two principal open-sided palm-thatched structures, the dining room and the bar. Spread like wings either side of this are just ten rooms, two of which would suit families or two couples, all slightly set back from the beach but giving directly onto it. Each is totally private and sits well apart from its neighbour: to escape completely ask for the remote room number 1, but accept the only downside is a good beach walk to dinner, albeit little hardship, guided by either the moon or the supplied 'shake' torch.

The generous rooms follow the theme and are effectively an open-sided structure with intricately detailed soaring roofs; walls of

at a glance

Airport	Dar es Salaam, or via Pemba (Mozambique)
Airlines	Emirates, British Airways, Swiss, Qatar Airways, South African Airways, KLM, LAM
Transfer time	2 hrs, 20 mins flight from Dar, 1 hr from Pemba, 25 mins by jeep
Rooms	13 (including 5 x 2-bed family villas)
Staff ratio	7
Activities	Guided snorkel, fishing, turtle hatching, dhow cruise, kayaking
Services	Wi-fi in bar
Other	Mobile phones (intermittent)
Children	Any age
Power type	3-pin UK
Currency	US dollar
GMT	+3
Booking	www.diveinstyle.com

screening peel back to afford views of the ocean, or close to provide privacy, while still allowing the dappled sunlight and wind to enter. The vast bed dominates the room and is set within a muslin-screened canopy, effectively a room within the room, where you can lie and sleep, lulled by the wind and shushing sea eating at the beach feet away, knowing what amazingly few bugs there are will not disturb you. A vast single slab of marble dominates the bathroom, with contrasting hewn marble basins, desk area and masses of cupboards. An expansive and partially covered deck with loungers, sofa and free mini bar completes your home.

This is simple luxury, not in the sophisticated and cosseting Six Senses style, just simple. It's really just you and nature, with luxurious and incredibly comfortable rooms, a fabulous beach, utter peace and tranquillity with nothing to disturb you but a few birds and monkeys. The major activities are limited to lunch and dinner served overlooking the sea either at the restaurant or the new south beach bar on the opposite side of the island. The food is simple, fresh and delicious, the local chef taking incredible pride in his work – needless to say, local fish forms a major part of his repertoire, sashimi and sushi being a constant. It would be easy to be picky about the food, but just look at the sheer logistics of getting the produce and you will appreciate what is on offer.

The cleverly decorated bar has the feel of a colonial home with local antiques, wicker sofas, generous banquettes and has been artfully divided into a series of informal intimate nests with wide, comfortable sofas begging you to sprawl on them for evening drinks. To one end is the small bar and quite often in season, while waiting here for dinner, you will be interrupted by the arrival of a rattan box of baby turtles appearing not unlike a plate of canapés; guests are invited to release them close to the sea. Guided by the moon, they swim amazingly strongly to their fate – before you become too sentimental, less than one in a thousand grow to maturity.

It would be going too far to say this is a diving hotel, as there are other activities, but they are limited. A picnic on a remote beach, a dhow cruise, deep-sea fishing, kayaking, but you come here just to chill, perhaps after a safari, with only the rustle of the sea and the endless busy chatter of the weaver birds to disturb you; or you come to dive, and the latter is worth the trip alone.

The dive school follows the theme of the resort, simple but perfectly organized. Situated close to the dining room, hidden away in the shade of the bush, it is here that all dive briefings take place. The mostly Scubapro gear is all in peak condition. However, I would recommend you bring your own mask as no resort I have ever visited provides anything worth looking through.

DIVE CENTER

Boats are simple open RIBs offering no shade, which is fine for the local sites a few minutes away, but not for the more distant ones. A brand new 9-metre boat with shade and better seating has recently arrived and this should radically change the dynamics, comfort and reach and may indeed open up other more distant sites yet to be discovered. While there have been changes since I visited, I can only say that at the time the entire operation was seamless and I can only hope that the new instructor matches this level of professionalism. Given the amount of effort and thought that went into establishing the basics of a simple but efficient operation in the first place, I have no reason to doubt this.

Dives are at 10 a.m. and 3 p.m., if local, or 9 a.m. if more distant, such as Neptunes. Either way you have ample time for a relaxed lunch at the hotel. The dive school is just ten metres from lunch and by the time you get there for the briefing you will find all your gear already on board. Like many safety conscious resorts, essential given the remote location, they will insist that every diver does a check dive to confirm your basic skills, regardless of your experience; understandable if you are to be cleared for Neptunes. While the new boat has a ladder to board, on the smaller boats be prepared for a very inelegant seal-like return. In short, the operation, not unlike the resort itself, is simple but works well; the local team headed up by Paul take care of everything.

at a glance

Boats	28-ft (wet, partly covered) and 19- and 25-ft wet RIBs
Group size	4–6
Instructors	1
Languages	English, French, Italian, Spanish
Courses	All PADI
Children	12+
Other	Computer hire, gear prep and wash down, night dives

ABOVE
Apparently sloathish lionfish are
voracious predators.

Vamizi is not a one trick pony, but nonetheless, I have
to focus on one dive, the aptly named 'Neptunes Arm'.
A 40-minute boat ride away (accompanied by humpback
whales and a glimpse of mating turtles) lies a sunken
island whose surface is about eight metres down.
Swept by currents, this is not a dive site for the easily
intimidated or indeed novice diver (you do need an
advanced ticket to partake).

DIVING

Dropped in the blue, you need to do a negative entry so you can
get down quickly; allow yourself to be distracted by the startling
fields of coral and you will not make it. Once in the protection
of the wall, which is actually the end of Fraggle Rock, a world-
class wall dive, you round the corner to – visibility permitting –
an awe-inspiring sight. Rising vertically out of the depths is
a series of somewhat foreboding and intimidating towering
pinnacles literally groaning with fish. An incessant waterfall
of long-nose emperors and snappers in their thousands tumble
from the peaks while some 30 grey reef sharks patrol their
domain. Giant potato cod, upwards of 300lbs glide through
the gulleys, and all this is set against a constant backdrop of
perfect corals, schools of batfish, giant kingfish and a stardust
of goldies. The final minutes are spent drifting with the current,
pouring over a field of perfect shallow coral, littered with colourful
flatworms and nudibranchs.

In short, I may have been lucky as I had perfect visibility (100 ft+),
but I can say no more than this was the dive of my life, the more
so when you realize that there is no one else for miles around –
a true privilege. By the time you read this I will have returned
because surely this secret cannot stay hidden. I have dived many

at a glance

Local sites	12
Level	Easy to advanced (proof required)
Visibility	75–150 ft
Must-dives	Neptunes Arm, Fraggle Rock
Snorkelling	Guided snorkelling, 12 local sites
Wetsuits	3mm in summer, 5mm in winter
Coral	Excellent, hard and soft
Marine life	Humpback whale, barracuda schools, giant kingfish, giant potato bass, grey reef shark schools, hammerhead shark, bumphead parrotfish, massive schools of long-nose emperors and snappers
Other	Hyperbaric chamber in Zanzibar

OPPOSITE, ABOVE, LEFT
A resident hallucinatory
school of Moorish idols at
Fraggle Rock.

OPPOSITE, ABOVE, RIGHT
Giant, really giant, grouper
patrol the canyons.

OPPOSITE, BELOW
Superb hard and soft corals
with the inevitable anthias.

ABOVE

Colourful flatworms and slugs
are common and in all different
colourways (below and bottom)
– fabric designers take note.

ABOVE, LEFT

A waterfall of snapper flows fro[m]
pinnacle to pinnacle.

LEFT

There is a resident school of 20 t[o]
30 grey reef shark.

BELOW
Beautiful leopard and tiger cowries are tempting to pocket, but please don't.

RIGHT
Hidden in this pristine coral head is the distinctive wavy dorsal fin of a leaf scorpionfish.

MIDDLE
A school of barracuda.

BELOW, RIGHT
The interior of clams is always worth a close inspection for the amazing colours.

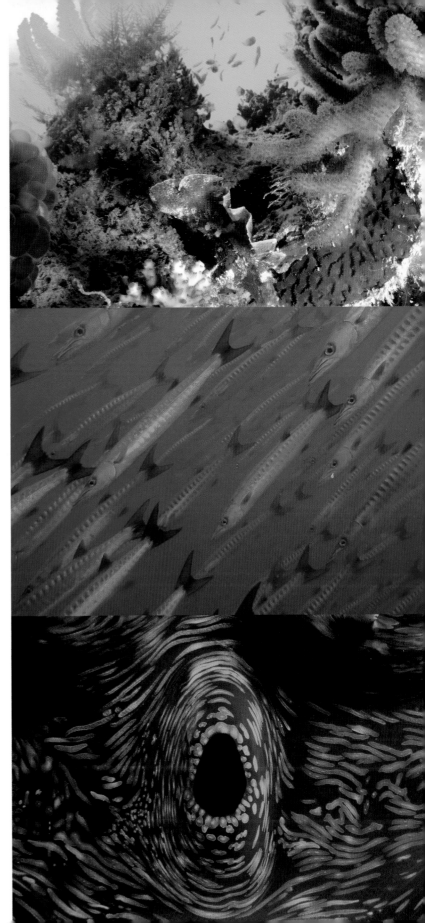

sites that claim to be in the world's top 10 and this was the first not to disappoint.

Aside from Neptunes, another must-dive is Fraggle Rock, a world-class wall dive swept by currents with its hallucinatory school of moorish idols which end up sweeping you into Neptunes Arm. To add to the joy of the dive, I was lucky enough to drop in on top of a pair of hammerhead sharks, a rare sighting, but evidence that they are here.

The diving here is incredibly varied, ranging from the long pristine gentle house reef which you can graze over, to the more alarming but exciting Neptunes Arm and if there was ever any encouragement needed to do your Advanced PADI, the prize of Neptunes should suffice.

As well as the Neptunes there are sites closer to home: Skunk Alley, Cave Wall aka the House Reef, which offer really gentle, easy diving with excellent corals, turtles, schools of barracuda, nudibranchs and all the usual suspects and given the variety and sheer quantity of marine life in these seas you are very likely to be surprised.

There are now just three hotels on Benguerra Island's 20 square miles, and the one that occupies the prime position on the west coast is Marlin Lodge. Built in 1995, it was originally the fishing lodge of a wealthy South African enthusiast who was drawn by the unparalleled game fishing in the surrounding waters. Where fishermen lead, divers often follow, and from these humble beginnings, the lodge has reinvented itself as a fully fledged boutique resort.

HOTEL marlin lodge

Creating accommodation like this in such a remote location is a feat in itself. Doing it twice is tiring, but as nature decided to rearrange the furniture with a cyclone in 2007, the owners had no choice, and took full advantage to shed its fishing lodge roots and convert it into a luxury resort. Benguerra is not a private island, and this is no bad thing: unlike many sanitized, fenced-off resorts, Marlin Lodge is very much a part of the local scene. Fishermen visit to trade their catch, the occasional local wanders the beach balancing a bundle on their head, and traditional dhows drift past in the gentle wind.

There are now just 17 rooms, spread along a berm of sand just behind the beach. All overlook the ocean and are reached by a timber walkway raised above the local flora and fauna, which gives you both a cool breeze and views of the island. The former Classic Chalets with their fishing past have gone, replaced with the far more spacious and sumptuous Luxury Chalets.

In addition to these there are just three Executive Suites, basically upscale versions of the chalets, with larger bathrooms and both indoor and outdoor showers. The interior walls are clad in a light beige fabric that emphasizes the feeling of space, while a four-poster bed draped in mosquito netting is perfectly positioned to

at a glance

Airport	Vilanculos via Johannesburg
Airlines	British Airways, South African Airways or Virgin Airways to Johannesburg, then Pelican Air to Vilanculos
Transfer time	7 mins by bus then 25 mins by boat
Rooms	17 (some air-conditioned)
Staff ratio	3+
Activities	Swimming pool, fishing, village tours, island picnics, walks, sunset cruise, full range of watersports, Wellness Center (small spa), business center
Children	14+
Power type	3-pin round
Currency	Mozambican metical (US dollar, euros, sterling and South African rand accepted)
GMT	+2
Booking	www.diveinstyle.com

give you the best views over the shady deck and the ocean beyond. Great care has been taken to ensure that the buildings blend into their natural setting and provide total privacy, however, do note that rooms 1 and 2 may be a bit too close to the main hub of the hotel if noise is an issue for you.

The newly decorated reception, bar and restaurant are housed in interconnected structures with a soaring reed-thatched roof. They offer a compelling combination of modern Western and traditional Mozambican elements: polished timber floors, honey-coloured timber railings, a local hardwood bar, and deep, comfy sofas for lounging and taking in the sights of the sea and newly enlarged pool. The restaurant lets you dine in both the shade and the open air, but every few days you will find the furniture missing, transported to the beach for a barbecue around a roaring bonfire. Unsurprisingly, the menu is built around fish (a set menu offers alternatives), and the food is served by smiling, attentive and mostly local staff. A waiter is assigned to you throughout your stay, so help is never far from hand.

Most guests seem to spend their time either by the pool or on the beautiful white-sand beach. For the horizontally inclined, the beachside Wellness Center now offers an enhanced range of massages and beauty treatments. Adventure-seekers can take advantage of the truly amazing fishing; there is also a Hobie Cat and a full range of watersports available, although the more leisurely inclined might prefer a sunset cruise. Pansy Island, just north of Benguerra and named for the pansy shells or sand dollars that wash up on its giant sand banks, is the perfect spot for lunch or a break between snorkelling or diving; en route you can visit a flock of flamingos or, if fortune favours you, you might even spot a few humpbacks or dolphins.

Marlin Lodge is something of a triumph in a country that until just a few years ago was riven by civil war. Things are only going to get better. As it stands, there is no more comfortable or stylish way to enjoy the wonders of the beautiful and remote Bazaruto Archipelago.

Housed in an immaculate thatched building next to the bar, the dive center offers an extensive selection of equipment and an even more impressive range of knowledge. An instructor can make all the difference to your diving experience, and in these waters there is no one better than Paul, a veteran diver of the archipelago, and his continued presence is one of the prime reasons I still recommend Marlin over newer contenders.

DIVE CENTER

Since there is just one guide, groups can be as large as the maximum of eight. Nonetheless, groups of three or four are common as the majority of guests come here for the deep-sea fishing, which is reputed to be the best in the East Indian Ocean.

As with virtually every destination in this book, your gear is taken care of until the end of your stay. It can be a bit of a walk to the boat when the tide is out, but this is no great hardship when you're treading on soft white sand carrying only your towel and, at worst, your dive computer.

There is an extensive range of diving vessels, from a purpose-built high-speed open boat to a fleet of modern, shady catamarans. This gives you a choice of speed, ideal for nearer sites, or comfort, excellent for day trips or going further afield.

One of the great advantages of diving at Marlin is that snorkellers can join many of the trips. Divers can venture outside of Two-Mile Reef while snorkellers stay within it; they can then meet at Pansy Island, a huge sandbar surrounded by turquoise waters and calm inlets, and a great place to picnic or while away a surface interval.

at a glance

Boats	21 ft+ (wet covered, dry covered)
Group size	8
Instructors	1
Languages	English
Courses	All PADI
Children	14+
Other	Food and drinks, gear prep and wash down, private charters, deep swimming pool suitable for training

This is unspoilt diving at its very best. The Bazaruto Archipelago is protected as a national park: there is no large-scale fishing here, just sport-fishing outside the boundaries. Thus the reefs are exceptionally healthy, particularly the soft corals, and the range of sea life is not only vast but also remarkably approachable.

ABOVE
There is a wide variety of incredibly cute, colourful but reclusive boxfish.

DIVING

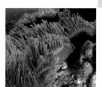

About halfway between the two major islands of Bazaruto and Benguerra lies Two-Mile Reef, the main, but not the only local dive site for Marlin Lodge. The sheltered side is excellent for snorkelling, while the ocean side offers some fantastic diving. The ocean floor is fairly shallow, maxing out at roughly 65 ft, so long dives are an option. Due to the reef's length and Paul's expertise, you can always find part of it to dive, practically regardless of currents – not that they're particularly strong to begin with.

Visibility averaged at around just 50 ft when I dived, but what could be seen was still impressive. The gently descending seabed provides hundreds of caves and gullies, some of which conceal 11-ft nurse shark (worthy of an entire Discovery Channel documentary) as well as white-tip shark. The flood tide can bring clear water along with enormous schools of barracuda, trevally and the occasional kingfish, but there is always an endless procession of tropical fish, set against a soft-coral reef background reminiscent of an underwater flower stall.

Honeycombs, the most passive of morays, are plentiful; some giant ones seem to know Paul and will accept a scratch. There are also schools of orange-spined surgeonfish hanging around coral heads,

at a glance

Local sites	12
Level	Easy to advanced
Visibility	50 ft+
Must-dives	Cabo San Sebastian, Two-Mile Reef
Snorkelling	Very good from dive boat
Wetsuits	3mm (5mm May–August)
Coral	Good, especially soft
Marine life	Whale shark, devil ray, manta ray, honeycomb moray, loggerhead, green and hawksbill turtle, guinea-fowl moray, large nurse shark, kingfish, barracuda, giant potato grouper, hammerhead, eggshell cowrie, schooling surgeonfish, schooling bannerfish
Other	Marine park, night dives, day trips, hyperbaric chamber in Durban (2 hrs)

RIGHT
The beautiful blue-spotted stingray is a common resident of Benguerra's waters.

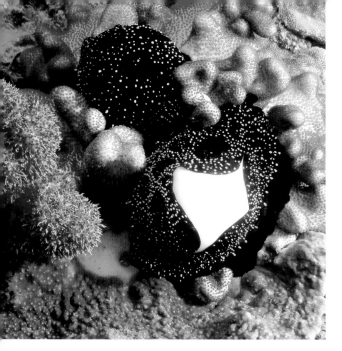

LEFT
It is becoming difficult to find large, living shells anywhere in the world, but stunning eggshell cowries abound in Mozambique. Their black mantles are a striking contrast to their white shells.

ABOVE
The bizarre but beautiful sea apple, a type of nudibranch, looks similar to a cardinal's hat.

ABOVE
The docile honeycomb moray is a common sight.

various nudibranchs including the amazing sea apple, crocodilefish, congregations of eggshell cowries, lionfish, swarms of glassfish, boxfish, white-spotted porcupinefish, blue-spotted ray, guineafowl moray, hawksbill, green and loggerhead turtle, carpets of anemones and their Nemos...the list goes on. And, during summer from November to March, you're bound to encounter the elusive whale shark, which arrive in droves along with manta and devil ray.

More experienced divers can go to Cabo San Sebastian, a fisherman's paradise that starts at 100 ft. Well over an hour from the lodge, it can only be found with the help of GPS, and while gearing up you can see the waters churn around you with schools of game fish. There is no distinct reef edge here, more like a gently descending current-swept plain, partially forested by green tree corals. Every now and then, the plain is broken by shallow gullies that hold sea life hiding out of reach of the current; it's wonderful to behold all manner of life slowly revealing itself, from lionfish and 3-ft-long potato cod to grey reef shark, hammerhead and huge turtles.

The surface interval is just as rewarding. I spent mine trawling under the stewardship of professional fisherman Jonathan, whose every move seems like a ballet. In no time at all, I worked my way up from plastic bait to a large yellowfin tuna, which I next met as sashimi at the bar.

BELOW
There is no shortage of sea life in the Bazaruto Archipelago.

Relaxed schools of orange-spined
surgeonfish populate the many
coral outcrops.

Small, soft corals literally cloak
the reef like a flower stall.

Bannerfish rarely travel alone.
Usually they swim in pairs or
schools.

The reptilian stare and Zen-like
calm of the crocodilefish make it
worthy of its namesake.

A thousand miles off the coast of east Africa en route to nowhere, the Seychelles are one of the most pristine and scenically stunning places on earth. They offer a rare blend of topographic beauty, stylish hotels and delicious cuisine; mix this with great diving and you have an irresistible cocktail. Even the most enticing brochures fail to do this far-flung archipelago justice, with its white beaches, crystalline waters and striking boulder formations, all set against a backdrop of lush vegetation.

The Seychellois government realizes how much this politically stable republic has to offer, but also how little – tourism is its lifeblood, and the nation depends on it to survive. The Seychelles' fragile natural beauty is their most powerful drawcard, and the authorities have fully faced up to the need to protect it. There are strict controls on new hotels and almost 50 per cent of the islands' land mass has been designated as nature reserves and national parks; luckily for divers, no less attention has been paid underwater. In this far-sighted way, the country is continuing to attract the visitors it needs while ensuring that tourism will never get out of hand.

The Seychelles comprise 115 white-lipped atolls and islands spread over almost a million square miles. Mahé is where you land, but it is the necklace of surrounding islets that best typify the staggering beauty of this island group. Here you will find the extraordinary Frégate Island Private

Frégate Island is a tiny speck on the edge of the Seychelles archipelago. This 740-acre jewel is home to a beautifully integrated boutique hotel, Frégate Island Private, where man lives in total harmony with nature. Turtles lay their eggs on its sublime beaches, the endangered magpie robin will join you for breakfast at your villa and you can even adopt one of the giant Aldabra tortoises that are raised and released into the wild on the island.

frégate island

HOTEL frégate island private

Since I last visited Frégate has moved the game on. The 16 Balinese-inspired villas, perched on granite rocks above the whitest sand imaginable now boast their own private infinity pool and jacuzzi; one even has its own mini spa. The line between indoors and outdoors is blurred: with full-length windows, a pool and terrace on one side and the ocean on the other, it's like being on a boat. You're free to enjoy the silent air-conditioning, but nothing compares to cooling off in the gentle tropical breeze with the sound of the waves below.

Although there is no direct beach access, you can walk or take your own solar-powered golf buggy to one of the island's seven *anse* (the Creole word for beach). The hotel beach is a wide expanse of soft sand that offers a bar, lounge chairs and excellent service. If clothes aren't your thing, then head to Anse Maquereau; just flip the sign over to read 'Beach Occupied' and it will be yours for the day. The best beach of all, however, is Anse Victorin. A perfect strip of white powder lined with palm trees and flanked by massive granite boulders, it embodies everything the Seychelles are about.

Meals are served literally wherever you like: your room, on the beach, at the restaurant, the new Tree House, the Jungle or the outdoor Pirates Bar carved into the hillside. The ever-changing menu is delicious, all

at a glance

Airport	Mahé
Airlines	Air Seychelles, Emirates, Qatar, Air France
Transfer time	20 mins by helicopter or light aircraft (24 hrs)
Rooms	16 (all air-conditioned) now with private infinity pools (2 with 2 beds)
Staff ratio	7+
Activities	Sailing, eco walks, bicycles, golf on Praslin Island, deep-sea fishing, canoeing, swimming pools, tennis, spa, gym, kids' club
Services	Internet, telephone, television, CD and DVD player
Other	Mobile phones
Children	All ages
Power type	UK 3-pin square
Currency	Seychelles rupee (all hotel bills must be paid by credit card)
GMT	+4
Booking	www.diveinstyle.com

fruit and vegetables being organically grown on the island. Dinner is sometimes served at the old plantation house close to the marina, which offers a welcome change of scene – driving there by buggy gives you a real sense of going out for the evening. Wherever you eat, informality is the order of the day, and there's not a jacket in sight.

If you've had enough of your villa or the beach, there is plenty to do, from climbing the peak of Mount Signal to taking a tour of Frégate's nursery for giant aldabra tortoises. There is also a small newly refurbished marina offering everything from canoes and windsurfers to private charters. If that sounds too energetic, you can escape to the truly amazing Rock Spa, a hilltop oasis set among lily ponds that offers a huge range of therapies, including a treatment based on coco de mer or sea coconuts, found only in the Vallée de Mai on nearby Praslin Island. There are few more relaxing ways to end the day than having a reflexology massage on an outdoor daybed while you watch the sun set and the terns wheel overhead for as long as your eyes stay open…

Frégate is a truly extraordinary place. It's the closest you will come to having your own private island and amazingly it is now well on the way to becoming carbon neutral. It seems you *can* have your eco cake and eat it.

Frégate is one of the only resorts in the Seychelles with its own marina – important given the seas that sweep these exposed islands – so your boat is just a stroll away from the immaculate newly rebuilt dive center. A small wash-down pool hints at the way diving is done here: on such a personal scale that they will not take more than two guests at a time unless you request otherwise. Not only will you not be crowded on your dive, but you certainly won't meet any other divers.

DIVE CENTER

The newly overhauled boats have a dedicated dry area for towels and cameras. Yours might be anything from a 31-ft purpose-built dive vessel, fine for calm seas, to the 41-ft-deep, V-hulled *Frégate Bird*, which offers a stable, comfortable platform in rougher conditions. The relaxed but thorough briefings take place on land, and you'll find your gear waiting for you on board, fully prepared and ready for your dive.

The dive center's equipment is replaced every two years and is always in first-class condition. The chances are you will not need a computer as the diving here is fairly shallow and tanks are small at ten litres. Nonetheless, you might want to bring one along if you're thinking of doing one of the few deeper dives.

The members of the dive team are among the most experienced in the Seychelles and have discovered most of the dive sites themselves. While they tend to concentrate on the area nearby, you can also opt for day trips to the beautiful islands of Praslin, La Digue or Mahé.

All in all, this is as painless and as personalized as diving gets. If you want to pick up the basics or are a nervous diver, there is nothing less intimidating than learning one-on-one. Like the hotel, the diving here is strictly 'private'.

at a glance

Boats	31 ft+ (dry, covered)
Group size	2
Instructors	2
Languages	English
Courses	All PADI
Children	10+
Other	Food and drinks, gear prep and wash down, private charters

ABOVE
Granite boulders make for
dramatic underwater landscapes
with endless crevices to explore.

Before the 1998 El Niño, the Seychelles hosted thriving reef systems, packed with vibrant corals. Today there is little of that left, but the marine life is still teeming and varied. Frégate offers some of the best diving in the islands, with extraordinary underwater landscapes and some amazing and unusual species. If you feel more adventurous, then another 50 sites await further afield.

DIVING

ABOVE
A baby emperorfish, even
more beautiful when young
than as an adult.

RIGHT
A pair of juvenile geometric
moray eels.

There are about nine sites in Frégate's immediate locale, all under 15 minutes away. One of the great things about the diving here is that you're almost guaranteed to see what you're after – it's a bit like diving on demand.

The best example of what diving here is all about is Stingray Point. Don't be fooled by the apparent desert beneath you. This is home to the rare Indian Ocean walkman and the extraordinary shovelnose ray: fierce looks, shark fins and a threatening shark shape, but in reality a ray in shark's clothing – worrying to behold but totally docile, feeding on seashells and other sand-dwelling creatures. You can also expect to see the bowmouth ray, a rarer member of the same family, as well as manta ray and smaller life such as anemone crabs.

The seabed is for the most part a gently descending floor of sand, interrupted by the occasional bommie teeming with life: you might see a family of geometric, honeycomb or yellow margin moray on one, catfish and glassfish on another. And while you focus on the small, you could well be interrupted by the noise, literally the noise, of an enormous school of mackerel appearing out of the murk like something from *The Blue Planet*.

RIGHT
A school of juvenile striped
eel catfish seek safety in
numbers.

at a glance

Local sites	9
Level	Easy to advanced
Visibility	50–100 ft
Must-dives	Stingray Point, Lion Rocks
Snorkelling	Good (ask hotel for directions)
Wetsuits	3mm
Coral	Poor
Marine life	Indian Ocean walkman, eagle ray, schools of unicornfish, big eyes and mackerel, manta (November–January), bowmouth, shovelnose, fantail and porcupine ray, green and hawksbill turtle, honeycomb and guineafowl moray, reef sharks and nudibranchs
Other	Hyperbaric chamber at Victoria on Mahé (20 mins), day trips to Mahé, Praslin, La Digue, Marianne and Shark Bank

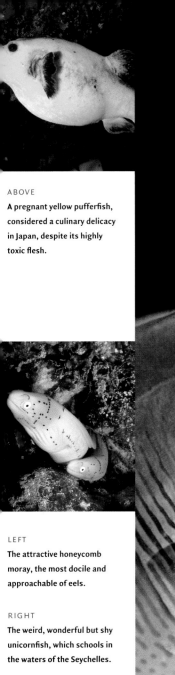

ABOVE

A pregnant yellow pufferfish, considered a culinary delicacy in Japan, despite its highly toxic flesh.

LEFT

The attractive honeycomb moray, the most docile and approachable of eels.

RIGHT

The weird, wonderful but shy unicornfish, which schools in the waters of the Seychelles.

ABOVE

ABOVE

A manta ray glides by at Stingray Point.

LEFT

Granite blocks from a giant's construction set are awesome to look at and provide shelter to many types of marine life.

ABOVE

A ray in shark's clothing: the extraordinary shovelnose ray.

BELOW

Curious and friendly Atlantic spadefish often accompany you closely on dives.

Lion Rocks, a field of dead coral that has clearly taken a
hammering from El Niño, again offers no shortage of sea life.
A more conventional-looking site is Surprise Rocks, whose
hard and soft corals are starting to make a comeback. However,
the real underwater architecture is created by the huge granite
boulders piled on the sea floor – you almost feel like a child
poking around a giant set of bricks. Exploring this rocky playpen,
you'll find enormous resting nurse shark, soaring devil rays,
boxfish, porcupinefish, green moray, lionfish, eagle ray, green and
hawksbill turtle, and the usual plethora of tropical fish. Friendly
batfish accompany you throughout the dive, occasionally nibbling
at your fins while you explore the endless nooks and crannies.
And these are just the local sites within minutes of the marina.

Snorkelling can be very good and will appeal to divers and non-
divers alike with plans afoot for an underwater walk! Provided the
seas are calm, the more intrepid can grab a glass-bottomed canoe
from the marina and pull it along as they snorkel off Airport and
Marina Beach. Alternatively, the dive center is happy to advise
guests about which beaches are best for snorkelling.

The diving here is very easy and suitable for all levels. The water
is not deep, nor is there much in the way of current, so it's an
ideal place for learners. An added plus is that on surfacing,
you are rewarded with the stunning sight that is Frégate Island,
a reminder of the luxuries that await you on your return.

maldives

Go now while you still can. These low-lying islands off the west coast of Sri Lanka will be among the first to disappear as sea levels rise due to global warming. The loss will be devastating, not only to the Maldivians but also to the 300,000 annual divers and visitors. These 1,190 unique jewels are strung out like a necklace from north to south, spread over some 500 miles of the Indian Ocean. Totally unspoilt, they offer a breathtaking sight from the plane before you even touch down.

Development here is strictly controlled, the maxim being 'nothing higher than a palm tree', and marine life enjoys similar protection as there is no real commercial fishing. Only 15 per cent of the islands are inhabited, with about a quarter of the population living on Male, so there are more than enough islands to go round between locals and visitors. Virtually wherever you go, you feel a million miles from anywhere.

There is a marked difference in diving between the northern and southern atolls, so it is worth trying to do both while you're in the region. Thankfully you won't have to compromise on accommodation: whether you venture to Soneva Fushi in the north or float around in the luxury *Four Seasons Explorer* in the south; there are few more desirable combinations. These exceptional destinations, along with the country that hosts them, are exactly what diving in style is about.

Soneva Fushi sits on the edge of the Baa atoll, a 30-minute seaplane ride northwest of Male. Ringed by perfect fine white sand and waving palms, it is large for a boutique hotel with over 60 rooms, but the beauty of this resort is that somehow it feels more like six. Your seaplane splashes down on a turquoise lagoon, and a three-minute *dhoni* boat ride later, your toes are plunged in pure white sand and you can say goodbye to your shoes.

HOTEL soneva fushi

If you have just bought a suitcase full of new Manolos to show off on holiday, this is not the resort for you. The very first thing you are handed on arrival is a 'No News, No Shoes' bag to store your footwear, and from then on, you will have only the sand between your toes.

First slightly disappointing impressions are of a few low, white-plastered structures set among palm trees, but these give way to the realization that true luxury comes in many forms. The place feels incredibly intimate, designed with meticulous care for the environment, and the natural, almost rugged aesthetic only adds to its charm. Husband and wife team Sonu and Eva (hence Soneva) have a very distinctive touch, which extends to Soneva Gili (pictured opposite, top right and bottom left), the sister resort in the eastern Maldives, which offers truly amazing overwater bungalows. Although the diving cannot quite match that of the Baa atoll, a few days there at the beginning or end of your stay are simply a must.

At Soneva Fushi, each room has its own character, and it is this lack of uniformity that makes the resort so special. Room sizes range from 500 square feet to over ten times that, but all benefit from the same comfort, flair and attention to detail: oiled timber floors, white-plastered walls accented by warm burnt-orange fabrics,

at a glance

Airport	Male
Airlines	Qatar Airways, Emirates, Monarch, Singapore Airlines, Austrian Airlines
Transfer time	30 mins by seaplane
Rooms	65 (all air-conditioned), some with private seawater pools
Staff ratio	4+
Activities	Fishing, watersports, table tennis, badminton, cultural excursions, tennis, volleyball, swimming pools (private), spa, gym (private), star observatory, champagne bar
Services	Telephone, television in some rooms, wi-fi, DVD and CD player, room service
Other	Mobile phones
Children	All ages
Power type	3-pin square
Currency	Maldivian rufiyaa, US dollar
GMT	+5
Booking	www.diveinstyle.com

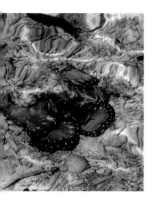

indoor and outdoor daybeds, bedside lights you can actually read by, a huge choice of pillows, endless fluffy towels and robes, massive bathrooms (some even float on their own lake opening onto a private garden with walls of waterfalls)... And just in case you need anything else, a team of over 300 smiling staff are on hand to oblige, headed by your personal Man Friday.

The island is criss-crossed by a network of sun-dappled sand paths (naturally brushed clear of leaves every day), which you can choose to travel either on foot or by bicycle. A handful of cosy shops are sprinkled along them, giving the resort the feel of a small village.

Meals are served in an increasingly original selection of outposts, be they up in the trees or with toes in the sand. The menu is astoundingly diverse, catering to all tastes, whether you fancy a hamburger, a spicy curry or anything in between. What's more, everything is faultlessly prepared. And for guests who have a sweet tooth, the island's own ice cream shop – unique among tropical resorts – offers no less than 64 different flavours.

Soneva Fushi is a very special place. Its owners continually strive to reach new heights. They dream it (star observatory, overwater champagne bar) then build it, upgrading villas, adding private pools, and incorporating new designs. It is simple luxury, or rather luxuriously simple. Every aspect nudges perfection.

Soleni Dive Center is perfectly run by Thomas and Alessandra, who have been at Soneva Fushi for over a decade. It works like a Swiss clock – appropriately, as Thomas himself is Swiss. This is probably the most experienced dive team in the Maldives, and its members are not so much instructors as underwater bush guides. They have an intimate knowledge of the reefs, and this makes the world of difference to your diving experience.

DIVE CENTER

There are usually two dives per day, at 9.30 a.m. and 3.00 p.m. The jetty is no more than 100 ft from the resort's main restaurant, so after filling up on breakfast or lunch, you only have a very short stroll to the boat. It's therefore worth taking along your camera, computer or whatever else you need when you leave your room in the morning.

The rest of your dive gear awaits you on board, freshly rinsed and dried by the ever-helpful dive team. A simple basket system is operated: your equipment is kept in a basket on the boat, and you simply put it back after your dive. Once you rig your own BCD, your tank is stored until you reach the dive site. The service is simply irreproachable.

The purpose-built dive vessel is a modern interpretation of a dhoni, with masses of deck space, a WC and a large sun deck laden with fat cushions. It makes day trips to the more distant reefs very enticing, especially as it cruises almost twice as fast as a traditional dhoni.

There are plenty of instructors with endless language skills, and diving in small groups is their speciality. They seem determined you should see everything and know the sites so well that you will not be disappointed. Interestingly, I dived the same reef with a different team and didn't see half of what Soleni showed us. I rest my case.

at a glance

Boats	35-ft luxury dhoni (dry, covered)
Group size	6
Instructors	5
Languages	English, French, German, Italian, Spanish, Japanese
Courses	All PADI
Children	10+
Other	Computer and underwater camera hire, dive shop, nitrox, food and drinks, private charters, gear prep and wash down
Website	www.soleni.com

If you were lucky enough to dive the Maldives ten years ago, you would have found them utterly spectacular. In 1998 they were devastated by El Niño, which is said to have destroyed 95 per cent of the region's coral. Thankfully nature is making an amazing comeback, largely thanks to the nutrient-rich currents that sweep the area. Soft corals are once again plentiful, while hard varieties, including cabbage and staghorn corals, are slowly but surely reappearing.

ABOVE
The Maldives were seriously hit by El Niño, but some areas have escaped. A rare piece of vibrant pink coral juts out from a wall.

DIVING

What has not changed is the sheer quantity and diversity of marine life. Diving the Maldives used to be truly magical, a real fairytale, but today it remains fantastic by anyone's standards. Here, on the Baa atoll in the north, you will come across everything from nudibranchs to manta ray, frogfish and stonefish – these islands have it all.

The only species in decline is shark, ruthlessly fished for their fins: every year a shocking hundred million of them are killed worldwide to cater to culinary demands in the Far East. The Maldivian government continues to permit this practice, and only whale shark numbers seem relatively unaffected. However, there are a few dive sites where shark do enjoy limited protection – here you can still find white-tip, grey reef, silky and, if you are very lucky, scalloped hammerhead shark. But by and large, divers will have to be content with species such as mantis shrimp, stonefish and Napoleon wrasse, whose lips are regrettably another Eastern delicacy.

The Baa atoll provides some of the easier diving in the Maldives thanks to its unusually wide channels, whose currents tend to be less severe than elsewhere; be aware, though, that the year's strongest currents are in January. That said, unless you go on a day trip, most of the dives you will do are on the local thilas or

at a glance

Local sites	12
Level	Easy to advanced
Visibility	50–70 ft May to November (wet season), 70–100 ft+ December to April (dry season)
Must-dives	Nelivaru Thila, Daravandu Thila
Snorkelling	Very good on house reef
Wetsuits	3mm
Coral	Recovering, soft better than hard
Marine life	Manta and eagle ray, whale shark, black-tip and grey reef shark, Napoleon wrasse, moray (4 varieties), pilot whale, frogfish, mantis shrimp, ghost pipefish, large schools of surgeonfish, snapper, trevally, jackfish, barracuda, batfish and unicornfish
Other	Day trips, night dives, marine park, hyperbaric chamber (20 mins)

OPPOSITE, TOP
The reefs are filled with unusual fish, including this tiny red frogfish.

OPPOSITE, MIDDLE
Anemone crabs live within the safety of the stinging tentacles of anemones. They extend their fine fans to sift the ocean for food.

OPPOSITE, MAIN PICTURE
The coral may have been badly damaged by El Niño, but this has clearly had little effect on the sea life. Here, on a single coral head, you can see a yellow margin moray, giant green moray, lionfish and marbled shrimp. Believe it or not, just out of the frame there is also a honeycomb moray.

OPPOSITE, BOTTOM
The reclusive mantis shrimp is armed with a powerful club that packs the force of a .22 bullet. It can, and has broken masks, camera lenses and even aquariums.

submerged reefs, more protected from the currents. Although there
is a lack of landmarks, Thomas and his crew seem to have no need
of GPS, and unfailingly take you to these invisible *thilas*, which rise
to within 15–30 ft of the surface. Chances are you won't experience
a poor dive; the Soleni dive team know exactly where to go and when.

A favourite destination is Nelivaru, perhaps because it is so close
to Soneva Fushi. In season this is a manta cleaning station, but
even out of season it has a lot to offer. Fans of moray won't be
disappointed: on a single coral bommie, a tiny underwater island
surrounded by sand and no more than 20 ft around, you might find
no fewer than three different species of moray, giving the bommie
the look of an underwater Hydra. With help from the Soleni team,
you can try and seek out the beautiful harlequin shrimp, a bit like
a taunting supermodel who shows you just enough to tempt you,
but holds much, too much, in reserve.

Wherever you dive, you will come across an astonishing diversity
of life: turtles, frogfish, porcupinefish, spotted, green and black-
cheeked moray, hawkfish, lionfish, clownfish, endless anemone,
ghost pipefish, scorpionfish, stonefish, pufferfish, schools of snapper
and fusilier, boxfish, jackfish, emperorfish, mantis shrimp, stingray,
eagle ray... all these and more are regulars to these waters. Thomas
also tells me that they have recently opened up a new site for good
manta and whale shark sightings, but it is seasonally dependent.

The tourism figures say it all. Despite the effects of El Niño and the
tsunami of December 2004, the Maldives continue to be a magnet to
divers and other visitors. These natural setbacks have failed to spoil
the beauty of these islands, either above or below the water. You can
do no better than allow Soleni to show you the truth of this.

Four Seasons Explorer is hardly recognizable as a live-aboard. It is in fact a floating Four Seasons resort, with all that implies. Launched in 2002, this 128-ft catamaran has been skimming the turquoise seas of the Maldives to rave reviews. Cruises start and finish at the Four Seasons Kuda Huraa, voyaging to the northern and southern atolls dependent on the weather. One thing is certain: you don't have to be a diver to enjoy this seafaring adventure.

four seasons explorer

BOAT

four seasons explorer

The *Explorer* is arranged on just three levels and offers plenty of covered and open deck space. You'll find everything from a fully equipped dive zone to an extensive library, external bar, jacuzzi, spa, dedicated sun deck and dining room with plasma screen for video presentations of your adventures and basic marine biology talks.

The boat sleeps a maximum of 22 guests in the light, elegantly simple staterooms. Their main features are the luxurious signature Four Seasons beds and the wide panoramic windows, which give wonderful views as you journey through the islands. No detail has been overlooked, be it the new soft linens and towels, excellent storage space, or your own CD/DVD player and flat-screen television. Two lucky passengers can sleep in the ultimate bed on board in the form of the *Explorer* suite, spanning the full width of the ship and enjoying amazing panoramic views as well as their own private terrace.

Activities might include island tours, lunch on a remote sandbar or an evening barbecue on a deserted beach (the food is delicious), but you will still have time to swim, enjoy a massage or generally chill out. Perhaps the best indication of the *Explorer*'s appeal is that only 50 per cent of guests are divers. There is no live-aboard like it anywhere in the world.

at a glance

Airport	Male
Airlines	Qatar Airways, Emirates, Monarch, Singapore Airlines, Austrian Airlines
Transfer time	15 mins speedboat (3 and 7 night cruises), 30 mins seaplane (4-night cruise)
Rooms	10 plus 1 suite (all air-conditioned)
Staff ratio	2+
Activities	Village trips, watersports, island picnics, fishing, spa treatments, marine biologist
Services	Telephone, television, internet, DVD, CD player and MP3
Other	Mobile phones (intermittent)
Children	10+
Power type	3-pin square
Currency	Maldivian rufiyaa, US dollar
GMT	+5
Booking	www.diveinstyle.com

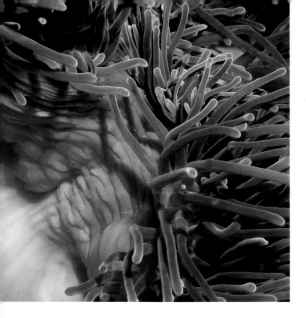

Just when you think things can't get any better than on board the *Four Seasons Explorer*, it's time to get into the water. Your diving experience will depend on the itinerary, but if you have already stayed at Soneva Fushi, it would be well worth trying for a cruise in the southern atoll. Wherever you go, you will experience the best of the Maldives, with the added bonus of diving a greater variety of reefs than you could staying at any one location.

ABOVE
The vivid colours of the
underside of an anemone.

DIVING

Four Seasons Explorer's spacious dive deck opens to the stern, where your neatly folded wetsuit awaits you. You can choose from an excellent range of dive gear, including flashlights and computers, and it's up to you whether you dive with nitrox or straight air. The dive sites can be anything up to 20 minutes away from where the FS *Explorer* anchors. This is no hardship, however, as you dive from a 30-ft dhoni, perfectly laid out as a dedicated dive boat. This gives you both shade and cover in case of poor weather and you can even have your tank refilled without returning to the mother ship.

Most dives are done in small groups, but sometimes they will verge on the larger side. Thus if size matters to you it's best to request a smaller group specifically; for a small premium, it is even possible to arrange for your own dedicated instructor. Normally there is a morning and afternoon dive, plus the occasional dawn or night dive.

Dives range from easy sites suitable for snorkelling to fairly serious drift dives. You can also explore some of the Maldives' main channels to the open ocean, increasing your chances of seeing manta and other pelagic life. Best of all, you get to dive an amazing diversity of sites. Going to bed in the luxury of a Four Seasons and then waking up in reach of brand new dive sites – this is a very special experience.

at a glance

Level	Easy to advanced
Visibility	50–70 ft May to November (wet season), 70–100 ft+ December to April (dry season)
Snorkelling	Good
Wetsuits	3mm
Coral	Recovering
Marine life	Manta and eagle ray, whale shark, hammerhead, white-tip, black-tip and grey reef shark, Napoleon wrasse, moray (4 varieties), pilot whale, frogfish, mantis shrimp, ghost pipefish, schools of surgeonfish, snapper, fusiliers, trevally, jackfish, barracuda, batfish and unicornfish
Other	Night dives, wreck dives, marine park in some areas, hyperbaric chamber

OPPOSITE, CLOCKWISE
FROM TOP LEFT
Scorpionfish, like stonefish, are masters of camouflage and some can even adapt their colour to suit their surroundings; the famous and almost iconic Shipyard wreck dive is great for exploring; the banded pipefish, small but perfectly formed; looking like a cross between a hamburger and something out of the *Muppet Show*, bivalves are a member of the clam family and while normally found moulded into the coral, do also have the ability to swim.

The island of Phuket lies just off the west coast of Thailand, a little over an hour from Bangkok by plane. In fact, it barely qualifies as an island – only a narrow channel of water separates it from the mainland – but it is ideally placed to deliver great diving. To the west it is washed by the warm waters of the Andaman Sea, and to the east is the protected Gulf of Phuket, home to the hauntingly beautiful Phang Nga Bay.

Best known for its beautiful beaches and some questionable sex ethics, Phuket will now always be remembered for the tsunami of Boxing Day 2004. Islands such as Koh Phi Phi were devastated, but in Phuket you have to stray from the usual tourist destinations to witness any of the damage. Now five years on there is little evidence of this disaster and the hotels are all back to normal, your final destination even more so, having been fettled, beautified and bettered in our absence.

Phuket is where you will find the very nucleus of Aman thinking, Amanpuri, and your holiday begins the moment you are met at the airport. Any stress from long-haul travel is sloughed off like an old skin while you relax into your Aman ride; a trademark cocoon of white slip-covered seats, lightly scented face towels and chilled Evian all serve as a taste of what's to come. Twenty-five minutes later, already soothed, you enter an almost private headland, home to just two hotels, *the* hotel being *the* incomparable Amanpuri.

Amanpuri was the trailblazer in the now ever-expanding Aman group. It was here, in 1988, that Adrian Zecha first realized his vision of a mouldbreaking style of hotel. Defying the naysayers, he took the concept of luxury to a whole new level, and his ideas now seem like a glimpse of the blindingly obvious. Today, aside from more mature vegetation, Amanpuri looks as if it has just opened, a testament to its timeless design and perfect upkeep.

phuket

HOTEL amanpuri

The centerpiece of the resort is the 100-ft infinity pool, now something of a trademark. This Zen-like expanse of midnight-blue water is devoid of clutter (the architect Ed Tuttle would not accept the aesthetics of umbrellas) and thus retains its architectural purity. When it was the drawing board in the 1980s it was truly revolutionary, and even today it is captivating. Perfectly reflected in it are the open-sided main buildings: the two restaurants, bar, reception and music pavilion, all overlooked by towering palms, a reminder of the site's former life as a coconut grove.

Forty rooms perch on the hillside, while 30 larger villas with their own pools lie hidden from view. Suspended on stilts, they are accessed by raised walkways and steep stairs, a modern interpretation of a traditional local village, but executed without the slightest hint of Disneyesque parody. It is simply incredibly stylish. These timber-clad structures are ideal for escaping the heat, the sound of birdsong undimmed by their silent air-conditioning. Built in Thai style with soaring roofs, they typify simple luxury. A spacious bedroom with an enormous double bed opens onto an equally expansive bathroom, while a terrace offers a shady chill zone or *sala*. The view varies, and as you would expect, the more of the ocean you want to see, the higher the premium: rooms 103 and 105, with a full sea view, will set you back twice as much as a garden room.

at a glance

Airport	Phuket via Bangkok, Singapore or Hong Kong
Airlines	British Airways or Thai Airways via Bangkok, Singapore, Hong Kong, Japan, Thai Airways to Phuket
Transfer time	25 mins by car
Rooms	40 suites, 30 villas (all air-conditioned)
Staff ratio	4+
Activities	Golf, rainforest, temple visits, watersports, tennis, new gym, spa, swimming pool
Services	Internet, telephone, room service
Other	Mobile phones
Children	All ages
Power type	2-pin flat or round
Currency	Thai baht, US dollar
GMT	+7
Booking	www.diveinstyle.com

The resort itself is spread across some 80 amphitheatre-like broad steps above the beach. The immaculate white-sand crescent is separated from a neighbouring hotel by massive granite boulders, giving you perfect privacy. The swimming is superb, with soft sand underfoot gently sloping to greater depths. White beaches can get very hot in these latitudes, but to give you an idea of the thought and effort that goes into an Aman, every morning a criss-cross network of cooling water is poured onto the sands. As a result, you won't need to hotfoot it uncomfortably from shade to shade.

Lunch is either at the casual beachside restaurant a few steps above the white sand, or now at the new Beach Club, complete with its own 20-metre pool (this time with umbrellas). Wherever you choose, dining is the very essence of tranquillity. The reflective blue-black waters mirror the tall palms and starlit sky, and you are softly lulled by traditional Thai harmonies drifting across from the music pavilion. Meanwhile, your taste buds are aroused by anything from traditional Thai cuisine to outstanding Wagyu beef, all perfectly prepared with spice levels tailored to your preferences. Amanpuri means 'place of peace' in Sanskrit, and this is nowhere more evident than at dinner.

Aman sees Amanpuri not only as their original resort, but as their flagship. While it does host the group's first dedicated spa, overseen by some of the best staff in the business, in fact there is little else to set it apart – every Aman is superb. Like all the resorts by this groundbreaking group, Amanpuri provides discreet luxury in incredibly uncrowded surroundings that subtly echo the individual country and environment. What's more, there is a staff-to-guest ratio that would give any hotel bean-counter a nosebleed. Each Aman is unique, reflecting the local culture and pampering you like nowhere else on earth. But Amanpuri will always be where it all began.

Unless you are learning to dive at Amanpuri, you will never know there is even a dive center. Once you have booked your dives, whether to the local reefs or the Similan Islands, all you have to do is let the reception know your size, and a selection of gear will meet you at the boat. It is utterly painless. The dive operation is run by the efficient H2O Sportz, and Amanpuri ranks at the top of their client list of five-star resorts. This means you do too.

DIVE CENTER

H2O Sportz has a vast array of vessels to choose from, depending on where you want to go and how large your group is – though there are never more than six people to a dive. A small, shady speedboat will get you to the nearer reefs, while a larger, faster boat will be called into service for day trips and overnighting.

Your departure point will depend on the weather; it can either be off the hotel beach, or from one of two harbours, a short drive away. It's easy to arrange a private charter, whether for a distant day trip or a brief outing, and drinks are always provided, with a full lunch for day trips.

A more adventurous choice is to charter one of the Aman fleet to overnight either north in the Similans or east in the Gulf of Phuket. A literal armada of boats is at your disposal, from the 23-ft *Sea Ray* all the way up to a 110-ft luxury fantail yacht. There is also a 40-ft junk, as well as what may be the most exotic of them all, the 90-ft *Maha Bhetra*.

Whether it is for one or two nights or more, chartering a boat enables you to dive more remote destinations and, best of all, to get there before anyone else. There is no better means to do this than on the *Maha Bhetra*, surely the most stylish way to dive these waters.

at a glance

Boats	20 ft+ (dry, covered)
Group size	6
Instructors	3
Languages	English, German, Russian; French, Japanese or Mandarin on request
Courses	All PADI
Children	12+
Other	Computer and underwater camera hire, nitrox and rebreathers on request, food and drinks, wash down, private charters
Website	www.diveh2osportz.com

The *Maha Bhetra* is a 90-ft purpose-built Thai cruiser, constructed to the exacting standards of Ed Tuttle, Aman's extraordinarily gifted architect. Each Aman resort is designed to capture the spirit of its country, and this luxury vessel is no different. There is nothing quite like her, and yet she is clearly Thai. You drift along at a stately eight knots, stretched out on an enormous daybed while some of the world's most dramatic island scenery slips by.

BOAT maha bhetra

Remarkably, this boat was featured in the very much land-based *Architectural Digest*, and you can see why. There are no visible concessions to adverse conditions. Never bound for Atlantic crossings or storm-tossed waters, her form is perfectly suited to gentle cruises over calm seas in a climate where there is a constant cooling wind. She would be unsaleable and virtually unusable in the Mediterranean or the Caribbean, but she is ideal for the Andaman Sea and the Gulf of Phuket. Here she has no equal – unsurprising, given such a bold and uncompromising design, and now she is even better, fresh from a refit.

Passengers dwell on two decks: the lofty upper deck, where you will spend most of your time on board, and the lower deck, which gives access to the cabins. There are just three air-conditioned double bedrooms, all beautifully finished in local hardwood and featuring a vast bed, generous shower area, vanity unit and masses of cupboard space. They open to the deck on both sides, with the master suite opening out on three sides. There are no corridors on this boat; you are always within view of the sea.

The upper deck is a covered, open-sided living space, offering a huge daybed, dining table and plenty of room for sunbathing. It is also home to the wheelhouse reminiscent of Jules Verne's

at a glance

Airport	Phuket via Bangkok, Singapore or Hong Kong
Airlines	British Airways or Thai Airways to Bangkok, Thai Airways to Phuket
Transfer time	25 mins by car
Cabins	3 (all air-conditioned)
Staff ratio	2
Services	Thai chef, fishing, canoeing, Thai massage therapist on request
Children	All ages
Power type	2-pin flat or round
Currency	Thai baht, US dollar
GMT	+7
Booking	www.diveinstyle.com

20,000 *Leagues Under the Sea*, complete with traditional brass wheel, angled glass and massive GPS screen.

As the sun drops lower in the sky, blinds can be let down for shade. The temperature is always perfect, a balmy wind constantly blowing from the east or west depending on the season – you'll never want for air-conditioning. Perched high above the sea, the experience is a bit like the seafaring equivalent of riding in a 4 x 4, looking at the world around you from your comfortably lofty vantage point.

You can take out the *Maha Bhetra* for up to seven days; it's up to you whether you venture north to the Similans, or southeast to Koh Phi Phi. Both routes offer amazing diving, but while the scenery in Phi Phi is dramatic, probably your best bet for diving is the Similans. The biggest advantage of even a one-day cruise is the chance to visit the dive sites before anyone else – you dive on your own. While there is no dedicated dive area on board, divers are very well catered for; if you don't dive or want a break from the water, then the daybed is an appealing alternative.

The best thing about the *Maha Bhetra* is that you are never separated from the beauty of the Thai islands; there is not so much as a sheet of glass to come between you and the surrounding scenery. The design is literally inside–outside, and you are protected from the sun and cooled by the winds, all the while being waited on hand and foot. This is surely the most sybaritic, stylish luxury you will find afloat.

Diving in Phuket is incredibly diverse, and Amanpuri caters to it all. While you can dive locally, you will be rewarded by venturing further on one of the hotel's fast boats to the Similan Islands, the finest diving Thailand has to offer. Here you will encounter stunning scenery, clear waters and 100-ft visibility; stay local and the visibility will be about half that.

DIVING

Day trips can be done either by private charter or in small groups. It takes about two hours to get to the Similans, normally only accessible between November and April due to weather conditions. The crossing may be challenging, but once you get there the lee of the islands offers extensive protection. Even if you are not a diver it's worth coming along – you might see leopard shark on the surface, for instance. Provided the weather cooperates, this trip is a must.

The Similans have some world-renowned dive sites with plenty of variety, from gently sloping walls to the east and dramatic boulders such as Elephant Rock to the west. Once subjected to dynamite fishing, the area has been a marine park since 1982, and it is now inhabited by a huge variety of life. There are some pristine reefs, thick with hard and soft corals, inhabited by green turtles, giant green moray, snowflake moray, yellow margin moray, octopus, leopard shark, cuttlefish, schools of anthias, pikefish, butterflyfish, lionfish and coral groupers, while jackfish and mackerel hover in the deep awaiting their moment. It's all here, and in the right season, you may even see whale shark and manta ray.

Closer to home are a number of sites, again accessible by day trip, the newest being five air force planes recently sunk only two

at a glance

Local sites	7 (for hotel)
Level	Easy to advanced
Visibility	50–80 ft in bay, 80 ft+ on west coast and Koh Phi Phi
Must-dives	Anemone Reef, Shark Point, Similan Islands
Snorkelling	Good on house reef and *Maha Bhetra*
Wetsuits	3mm
Coral	Excellent
Marine life	Leopard shark, ghost pipefish, seahorse, harlequin shrimp, yellow, snowflake, banded-ring and white-eyed moray, clownfish (5 varieties), whale shark, green and hawksbill turtle, manta ray (at Hin Daeng and Muang), shovelnose ray, schools of sea pike and yellowtail fusilier
Other	Day trips, night dives, wreck dives, 2 hyperbaric chambers in Patong Beach and Deep Sea Port

OPPOSITE, ABOVE, LEFT

The ornate harlequin ghost pipefish is one of the most delicate, beautiful and elusive of all marine species.

OPPOSITE, ABOVE, RIGHT

Scorpionfish are so well camouflaged that you can only see their colours with artificial light – watch out when looking for a handhold in a current.

OPPOSITE, BELOW

Anemones curl into a ball when they sleep, displaying their mouth and vividly coloured underside. Under a flashlight they take on an almost ethereal glow.

miles from Amanpuri beach and already attracting life. Anemone
Reef and Shark Point are absolute must-dives. The visibility may not
be perfect, but it hardly matters. The sites are on the eastern side of
Phuket, about an hour from the marina, and it is worth getting here
as early as possible as it does get busy.

Shark Point is where you go to find the beautiful leopard shark,
which in this protected zone is spared the barbaric practice of finning;
if you are lucky you will also find seahorses. Anemone Reef, nearby,
is perhaps even more rewarding. The reef itself is relatively small,
coming to within 15 ft of the surface, but there is such a profusion
of life that you simply cannot cover it all in a single dive. It is aptly
named: anemones create an all-enveloping cloak, clinging to every
surface. Waving back and forth in the surge, they reveal a myriad of life
beneath; ghost pipefish, endless varieties of moray, unusually coloured
scorpionfish, lionfish, giant map pufferfish, boxfish, nudibranchs,
staggering cowries...even if you spend days there, you may not see
more than half of it.

An added plus of diving the Gulf of Phuket is the extraordinary surface
scenery. It's hard not to find your surroundings jaw-dropping when
you surface, and whether you are a diver or not, you should spend
a day on the water just to behold the beauty of Koh Phi Phi, the
location for the film *The Beach*, and James Bond Island, among
others. The very best way to cover these dive sites is with a private
charter, on one of Aman's luxury fleet; this ensures you can dive at
dawn and have the site to yourself. Failing that, any of them are still
worth a day trip – just make sure to get there early. Surprisingly, even
after the terrible tsunami, the reefs are incredibly healthy and filled
with a wonderful variety of life. This is truly great diving.

Consisting of some 7,100 volcanic islands and islets, many of which don't even have a name, the Philippines seems to float on its own in the Pacific. Separated from Indonesia and Indochina by miles of ocean, its history is relatively undramatic; unlike many of its neighbours, it has not seen the rise and fall of dynasties. This may be due to the archipelago's linguistic, cultural and racial diversity – over 111 dialects are spoken in its various regions.

The Philippines has the distinction of being the only Catholic nation in Asia. This is thanks to the strong Spanish influence, which began when Ferdinand Magellan first set anchor here in 1521. While Muslim separatists on the island of Mindanao are a source of some much-publicized unrest, the great bulk of the country is peaceful. You're highly unlikely to notice these rumblings if you stay at Amanpulo.

Located on the private island of Pamalican in the middle of the Sulu Sea, Amanpulo is just an hour's flight south from Manila, but it feels a world away. Your stay in the capital may be no more than a brief interlude in the immaculate Aman airport lounge, but if your flights mean you need to spend a night there, then the Peninsula is the place to go. It's worth arranging for a car to meet you at the airport for the slow crawl into town, but do not be tempted to spend any more time than you have to in this urban sprawl – true luxury awaits you on Pamalican.

Amanpulo *is* Pamalican. The name means 'peaceful island', and it's easy to see why. Pamalican's 250 pristine acres are totally tranquil, with nothing but a luxurious 40-room hideaway, verdant vegetation, exotic bird life and what must be one of the planet's all-time greatest beaches, a seemingly endless stretch of the finest white powder sloping into clear turquoise waters.

pamalican

HOTEL amanpulo

Designed by a leading Filipino architect, the spacious *casitas* or rooms are inspired by the *bahay kubo*, a traditional thatched structure. The 29 beach casitas are incredibly private, discreetly hidden away behind the beach, while the 11 hilltop casitas are tucked further back, some with views towards the neighbouring island of Manamoc – rooms 39 and 40 offer stunning panoramas. In true Aman style, they all feature a huge double bed, two daybeds, a desk area and two walls of windows opening onto your own private deck with yet more daybeds. Rough pebble-washed walls, coconut-shell tables, timber floors and wicker blinds complete the interiors.

The main building comes into its own later in the day. Perched on higher ground, this single-storey expanse houses the library, bar and dining room, as well as an extensive boutique. There is also a truly enormous infinity pool, set about with well spaced-out umbrellas and private *salas* – like all Amans, Amanpulo dedicates so much space to each individual guest that you feel as if you're on your own. The secluded, open-sided salas are ideal for relaxing during the day (they all shelter a large, inviting daybed), but they are even better at night – the orchid-strewn pool sala being a simply amazing venue for a private supper. Wherever you dine,

at a glance

Airport	Pamalican via Manila
Airlines	Air France, Cathay Pacific, Japan Airlines, KLM, Emirates, Philippine Airlines, Qantas, Singapore Airlines
Transfer time	1 hr by plane
Rooms	40 plus 11 villas (all air-conditioned)
Staff ratio	5
Activities	Watersports, tennis, spa, yoga, swimming pool, fishing, sailing
Services	Telephone, television, room service, internet in club room, wi-fi, iPod dock
Other	Mobile phones
Children	All ages
Power type	2-pin flat
Currency	Filipino peso, US dollar
GMT	+8
Booking	www.diveinstyle.com

the service is always faultless, and the delicious food ranges from traditional Filipino to classic Western dishes.

As you would expect from its truly incredible stretch of sugar sand, Amanpulo gives you the ultimate beach holiday. There are all the watersports you would imagine, as well as private boat trips to neighbouring islands, and moonlight or sunset cruises. If you prefer to stay on land, you can explore the island from your own golf cart that meets you at the airstrip on arrival, and makes getting around utterly effortless. Just be sure to keep insect repellent to hand and the nik niks or sand fleas won't bother you.

Children are brilliantly looked after by carers, but not to worry if you don't have kids – the resort is so spread out that they are never intrusive. Meanwhile, in the background a delightful team of some 350 staff makes sure you never lack for a thing.

All in all, this is the unspoilt Philippines at its very best, in such complete contrast to Manila that it's hard to believe you are only an hour away. Whatever preconceptions you may have of this country, Pamalican, and specifically Amanpulo, totally rewrite them. The hotel remains something of a secret, but it now deserves to be a destination resort having really come of age and revealed its true potential. I think I need to return.

The original simple dive center is no more. Now moved round the point onto its own piece of pristine beach, a true Amanesque dive center has arisen, a five-minute buggy ride from virtually any of the casitas, a little further from the new villas. If you have brought your own gear, they will happily collect it for you, otherwise there is a good selection of Scubapro and Gull equipment available, including children's sizes.

DIVE CENTER

Dives are pretty flexible and you can choose from 8 a.m., 9 a.m., 10 a.m., 11 a.m., 1 p.m. and 3 p.m. Groups can include up to four guests, but usually you will find it is just you and your instructor. The dive team are international and have a good knowledge of the local reefs; they always sport a smile and seem endlessly enthusiastic about the diving here, regardless of how often they get wet.

You board the new dive boat from the almost private 'dive beach', a big improvement from its former location, with soft sand underfoot. The boat provides shade, though expect to get wet on board – not a problem, as you arrive at the dive sites in a matter of minutes; the new bigger boat with waterproof compartment is a major step up, but it is worth taking a waterproof bag if you want to keep your things dry. Snorkelling is well catered for, with regular trips out to the reefs where you are guaranteed to see masses of fish thanks to regular feeding. The more adventurous can make their own way by taking out a kayak and tying up to one of the designated buoys.

The service here is flawless. You suit up in the shade of the dive center and your gear awaits you on board, where you leave it after the dive. The wash-down service is exemplary; everything is professionally rinsed. It's a great place to learn to dive.

at a glance

Boats	27 ft+ (wet, covered)
Group size	4
Instructors	2
Languages	English, Tagalog
Courses	All PADI
Children	8+ (Bubblemaker)
Other	Computer hire, drinks, wash down, private charters

Pamalican is a self-declared marine park, a rarity in a country notorious for using dynamite and cyanide to catch fish on its reefs. There are two coasts to dive, the more sheltered western shore, where Amanpulo's main beach is situated, and the more open eastern one. The prevailing winds shift seasonally so almost regardless of weather there is always at least one shore available for diving.

DIVING

All the dive sites are a maximum of 15 minutes from the center. Few permit mooring, but you will always find the boatman waiting for you when you surface, regardless of weather conditions. Visibility varies, ranging from as little as 30 ft on the protected house reef up to 85 ft or more at Casita 40, where the open sea seems to clear things up.

Turtles nest on Pamalican and you are virtually guaranteed to see them whenever you dive these waters. The turtles are accustomed to human interaction: Amanpulo looks after their eggs and makes sure that the hatchlings are returned to the wild, and at the right time of year you can witness all of this. Even the house reef, an easy dive just off the main beach, boasts a number of giant green and hawksbill turtles – you might see one gliding by, as big as 6 ft from tip to toe, with its shell providing a comfortable ride to a pair of 3-ft-long remoras. The fish on the house reef are plentiful too, including blue-spotted ray and yellow margin moray, along with barramundi cod and their beautiful dancing juveniles.

Fan Coral is a dive of a different league. Its immaculate reefs provide home to a panoply of tropical life: lobster, clownfish, emperorfish, Moorish idol, Napoleon wrasse, endless blue-spotted ray and even

at a glance

Local sites	8
Level	Easy
Visibility	30–80 ft+
Must-dives	Casita 40, Fan Coral and The Tip
Snorkelling	Very good on house reef
Wetsuits	3mm
Coral	Very good
Marine life	Cobia, devil, eagle and shovelnose ray, manta ray (December), large green and hawksbill turtles, reef shark, large frogfish, stingray, tuna, flying gunard, blue ribbon eel, nudibranchs
Other	Night dives, marine park, hyperbaric chamber in Manila (2 hrs)

the odd giant stingray. This is one of the most appealing dives on
the entire island.

Casita 40, located opposite Amanpulo's casita of the same number,
is arguably Pamalican's top dive and it is worth diving here more
than once. A drop-off from 30 ft down to 130 ft, this is a thriving reef
where you will see enormous inquisitive cuttlefish, turtles and local
shovelnose ray. Soft corals seem to be everywhere, while massive
sea fans and table corals are making a particularly strong comeback
after the devastation caused by El Niño and a major typhoon.

The Tip is something of a surprise dive, filled with unexpected
pleasures. Here you can swim with devil ray within arm's reach. Eagle
ray and other pelagics may pass by, as well as white-tip and black-tip
reef shark, tuna, the inevitable gargantuan turtle, and even 5-ft-long
cobia. Another great site is the Windmill, located at the northeastern
end of Pamalican, facing Concepcion Island. While this drops down
to 120 ft, divers don't need to venture deep to enjoy its natural beauty.

While the Philippines' very best diving is further south at the
amazing Tubbataha Reefs marine park, this is only accessible
by live-aboard. Nonetheless, Pamalican comes close. Add in the
unimaginably perfect beach, a wonderful hotel, superb service
and total privacy, and you soon realize that this is as good as it gets.

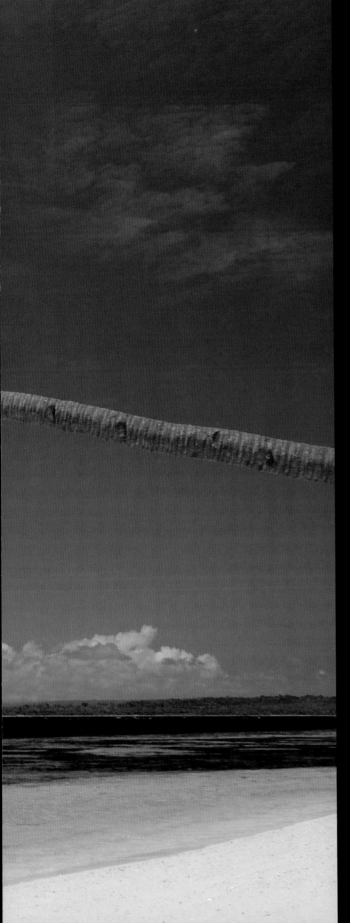

Indonesia

Indonesia is the world's largest archipelagic state, encompassing some 18,000 islands spread over a vast area. A third of these are uninhabited, and many of the rest host little more than a fishing village. In the more remote areas, it's hard to believe that this is the fifteenth most populous nation on the planet, with a population only 20 per cent smaller than that of the USA.

Independent since 1949, Indonesia is an amalgam of many island provinces and has only recently settled into being a democracy. Bali is almost a country within a country, a Hindu island in a predominantly Muslim nation, with one of the most beguiling local cultures in the world. Whether you stay on the coast or up in the hills of Ubud, you are immersed in the traditions of this almost mystical destination: scores of sacred festivals take place each year, when the whole island seems suffused with incense and strewn with flower petals. To top it off, you can stay at some stylish and luxurious hotels. No visit to Indonesia is complete without a trip here.

Travel a bit further, however, and you will find not only wonderful places to stay, but also the greatest underwater biodiversity on earth. Denpasar, Bali's capital, is a major regional hub and easily reached via Singapore and Bangkok. From here you can travel to Moyo Island, home to Amanwana, and on to the stunning waters of Komodo National Park and the newly arrived *Amanikan*, the first floating Aman. Alternatively, get a little more extreme at Wakatobi or on board the incomparable *Silolona*.

The remote island of Moyo encompasses some 2,500 acres and hosts a number of small villages, with a total population of only 2,000. On a protected cove in the west lies Amanwana, a secluded hideaway with 20 guest rooms, or rather 'tents'. These aren't just any tents, however. Designed by a Belgian architect to get around a local law dictating that no hotel structure could be permanent, they are a modern and utterly luxurious interpretation of the word.

moyo

HOTEL amanwana

Surrounded by mature tropical forest, Amanwana has no gardens as such, only a sheltered jungle clearing. Nature has been tamed enough to provide a smooth carpet of grass, but that's about it. Invisible birds call to one another endlessly, while playful monkeys scamper around the grounds, occasionally bouncing off your tent roof. You are on both a safari and a beach holiday – a kind of beach safari, with a generous helping of style.

Whatever foresight possessed the Aman group to buy this bay and build a hotel on such a remote island is a mystery, but we should all be grateful that they did. A seaplane will take you direct from Bali and deposit you at the hotel dock, or you can take a direct helicopter charter. From the moment you arrive, the magical Aman ingredients come into play.

If the last time you slept in a tent is an experience you're trying to forget, Amanwana will challenge your preconceptions. An elegant solid structure with a soaring canvas roof, it does a good enough imitation of a tent to satisfy the authorities, but you'd hardly recognize it on a campsite. You can choose between the Oceanfront and Jungle Tents; either is exceptional, but it's worth paying the small premium for the oceanfront tents' extra privacy and view. Both

at a glance

Airport	Denpasar
Airlines	Garuda, Japan Airlines, Malaysian Airlines, Qantas, Singapore Airlines, Thai Airways
Transfer time	1 hr direct flight
Rooms	20 (all air-conditioned)
Staff ratio	8
Activities	Trekking, kayaking, windsurfing, sailing, deep-sea fishing, small swimming pool, Jungle Cove spa
Services	Telephone, television, DVD lounge, CD player in music pavilion, room service
Other	Mobile phones
Children	All ages
Power type	2-pin round
Currency	Indonesian rupiah, US dollar
GMT	+8
Telephone	+62 371 22233
Booking	www.diveinstyle.com

will give you a huge bed festooned with mosquito netting, a desk, a luxurious open bathroom with twin handbasins and masses of storage space. There are also two L-shaped sofas that are perfect for an afternoon snooze, but also ideal for young children to bunk down on. The typical Aman touches are everywhere: a cotton island map, complimentary sarongs, bowls of exotic fruit, woven sun hats and baskets, all yours for the taking.

There are plenty of dining options. Lunch is informal, served either by the pool or at the open thatched dining pavilion. The simple menu changes daily, with a choice of delicious local and Western starters, main courses and desserts (if you can't take spicy food, you can always ask them to tone down the chilli). In the evening, you can dine at the main pavilion or, for a small premium, keep your toes in the sand by your tent, with your own private bonfire, a table surrounded by hurricane lanterns and a view of the setting sun.

At first glance there doesn't seem to be much to do aside from dive, snorkel or chill, but Amanwana ensures you won't be bored. For instance, the resort offers Hobie Cat cruises, guided jungle hikes and, most memorably, a trip to the island's waterfalls, best early in the year. You take a boat to the local fishing village, switch to African safari mode on an open jeep (take a hat and sunscreen), then walk until you reach the cool clear limestone waterfall pools surrounded by rainforest, where you can take a dip followed by lunch. At the end of the day, you can wind down with a massage at one of Jungle Cove's stone-built treatment rooms, open to the sky and sea.

Amanwana will not give you a beach holiday in the traditional sense. The sand is made up of coarse ground coral, while low tide reveals a craggy seabed. Coming here is about escaping the modern world; being on such an isolated outpost makes you feel like an adventurer, albeit one with more comforts than you can imagine. Most importantly, it's about enjoying the ocean. The water is totally clear and the temperature always perfect, so snorkelling is wonderful (or you can let the fish come to you on the jetty at the 3 p.m. fish feeding). Best of all, while here, you can explore the famed Komodo National Park on 28 metres of floating Aman, the *Amanikan*, the latest addition to the Aman experience.

Amanwana's dive center is located midway between the main restaurant and the dock, where all diving starts and ends. The facilities are fairly simple, but there is an excellent room for teaching and a pair of stylish outdoor showers. However, unless you are learning to dive, you will never need to come here once you have chosen your gear from the good range of Oceanic and Seaquest equipment on offer.

DIVE CENTER

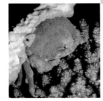

There is something of an armada of Aman boats available, but your main choice will be between a fast 26-ft Boston whaler and a much slower 45-ft traditional outrigger. The whaler is good for the more distant sites, while the outrigger, with plenty of shade and space for sunbathing, is ideal for a leisurely ride to the local reefs. The rest of the Aman navy means that you'll never be without a boat.

The dive team here is fantastic, and if you are lucky, then Kaz will be there to show you the reefs. He is a true underwater bush guide, able to spot things at a distance that you may find difficult to recognize even close up. Often his underwater horn will go off and you will swim to him, only to follow him even further to somewhere he thinks he has seen something. He always has, whether it's a camouflaged frogfish or a tiny nudibranch. Dive with Kaz and you will never miss out on any of the underwater action.

Even when Amanwana is practically full, you're unlikely to find many other guests diving. In fact, there may be as few as two of you along with one or even two instructors, all to yourselves. How long this place can remain undiscovered by divers is anyone's guess. For the moment, the dive center is something of a best-kept secret, and now is the time to take advantage of it.

at a glance

Boats	23 and 26 ft+ (dry, open/ covered)
Group size	4
Instructors	4
Languages	English
Courses	All PADI
Children	12+
Other	Computer and underwater camera hire, food and drinks, gear prep and wash down, private charters

The sites around Moyo are utterly superb and the coral gives Australia's Great Barrier Reef a run for its money. On top of all this is the most incredible underwater biodiversity anywhere on the planet – it's a true cradle of marine life. You can dive near or far, whether on the amazing local reefs or at more distant sites on day trips. Wherever you go, you'll find wonderfully pristine conditions, and you won't bump into any other divers.

ABOVE
The reefs around Moyo explode
with a blizzard of marine life.

DIVING

Amazingly, one of Moyo's best sites is just a few minutes from Amanwana. Even if you have dived the wonders of the Great Barrier Reef, there is something very special about Panjang Reef. If you have a camera, it's hard to know which way to point it – it's almost overwhelming. The stunning reefs are thriving with dense fields of hard coral – cabbage, staghorn, barrel sponge, sea fan, elephant-ear sponge – and there is no evidence of bleaching.

All this is covered in an undulating wall of marine life. On this dive alone you can see frogfish, nudibranchs, blue ribbon eel, lionfish of all sizes, scorpionfish, leafish, large brown moray and white-tip reef shark, along with a plethora of other species. An added plus of this dive is that although the reef rises from the sea floor some 160 ft beneath, its top is only 15 ft from the surface, so not a moment of your air is wasted as you explore its many wonders.

Snorkelling is truly excellent, either straight off the beach or from a dive boat on any of the reefs whose peaks almost break the surface. For the adventurous, Amanwana even offers night-time snorkelling – unheard of at most resorts. Speaking of which, if you have never done a night dive, then this is the place to start. A five-minute boat ride takes you to the old work jetty and the wreck of a timber

at a glance

Local sites	15
Level	Easy to advanced
Visibility	100 ft+
Must-dives	Panjang Reef
Snorkelling	Very good on house reef, excellent from dive boat; night snorkelling available
Wetsuits	3mm
Coral	Superb
Marine life	Blue ribbon eel, frogfish, leafish, nudibranchs, manta ray, whale shark, sunfish, white-tip and grey reef shark, schooling trevally, ghost pipefish, pygmy seahorse, bobtail squid, crocodilefish
Other	Night dives, wreck dives, marine park, hyperbaric chamber on Bali (2 hrs)

OPPOSITE, MAIN
PICTURE
There is so much to see that
it's easy to forget the little
things. It is always worth
checking for smaller life,
especially in anemones.

OPPOSITE, TOP
A night dive at Moyo is
particularly worthwhile. All
types of unusual life forms
come out to feed after dark.

OPPOSITE, MIDDLE
The tasselled scorpionfish
is a master of camouflage
and armed with venomous
spines, but is only dangerous
if stepped on.

OPPOSITE, BOTTOM
A pair of voracious lizardfish
wait for dinner to swim by.

boat, right off the beach. Here you might come across tiny ghost
pipefish, giant sleeping triggerfish wedged in their lairs, parrotfish,
scorpionfish, aggressively hunting fimbriated moray or even a clutch
of baby moray – all in just a few feet of calm water. Most remarkably,
you'll find nudibranchs the size of soup plates. These are something
of a revelation: nudibranchs tend to be a few inches at most, but
these enormous, almost black varieties (some with a white pattern)
are literally 12 inches or more in diameter.

There are a number of other dives around Moyo, all memorable for
different reasons: Tanjung Menagis for its amazing garden of soft
corals, unicornfish, silver-tip and white-tip reef shark; Angel Reef
for giant trevally, Moorish idol and red snapper; and the Wreck,
notoriously hard to find, a former fishing boat that is now home
to giant scorpionfish, lionfish, crocodilefish, boxfish, nudibranchs,
mantis shrimp and ringed pipefish.

It's impossible to see everything during a short stay on Moyo
Island. It's so easy to become so entranced by the reef that all
the larger life may well be swimming just behind you. Manta ray,
green and hawksbill turtle, sunfish, sailfish, whale shark…they
are all here, so seeing them is just a matter of luck. Luck aside,
you are guaranteed serene diving in wonderfully clear water with
no one else in sight, just some amazing sea life. And you get to
call the luxury of Amanwana home.

Named after the magical boat of a local legend, the *Silolona* was the brainchild of Patricia Seery, an American who lived in Indonesia for 20 years. With incredible determination, she saw her dream grow into an amazing marriage of traditional shipbuilding skills and the most up-to-date technology. The result is 150 ft of floating perfection. Since I last reported she has been fine tuned and her choice of destinations extended. There is no better way to dive, snorkel or just visit the remote islands of Indonesia: simple.

silolona

BOAT silolona

The *Silolona* is a *phinisi*, a type of boat built only by the Bugis in the mangrove swamps of Kalimantan, northern Borneo. Over a period of three years, with the help of just one chainsaw, a small electric sander and unbelievable skill, this remarkable craft morphed from hardwood trees in the local forest into 150 ft of stylish timber boat that now meets the highest German construction standards, more demanding even than those of Lloyd's Register in London. Its wooden beams are exposed so you are always aware that it is 'old', yet it offers every modern amenity, from full air-conditioning to an endless supply of hot water, all blended into the traditional design.

The salon has a sweeping 270-degree view and looks out onto the spacious teak deck, regularly washed down to keep it, and your feet, cool. With its banquette seating, intimate dining area and plasma screen for you to watch your adventures, this is the perfect retreat in case the weather ever turns against you. To add to the shady stern cushion-strewn dais, an new improved bow version has been added: this has to be the best vantage point at any time of day with just the hiss of the bow wave for company. You sleep below deck in one of five cabins, named after some of the islands that make up the Indonesian archipelago; all are spacious and equally comfortable, with elegant interiors, full double beds, beautifully fitted shower

at a glance

Airport	Denpasar
Airlines	Garuda, Japan Airlines, Malaysian Airlines, Qantas, Singapore Airlines, Thai Airways
Transfer time	3 mins from Amanwana by boat
Cabins	5 (all air-conditioned)
Staff ratio	2
Activities	Walking, island visits
Services	Massage
Children	All ages
Power type	2-pin round
Currency	Indonesian rupiah, US dollar
GMT	+8
Telephone	+62 371 22233
Booking	www.diveinstyle.com

rooms and good reading lights. Always trying to improve, this year the slightly troublesome generators I commented upon have been replaced with the most cutting-edge technology to reduce noise and vibration even further; this means Bali would probably be my cabin of choice.

The service and the food are the final flourishes. You are hardly aware of the boat's crew of 16 locals, who genuinely seem to take pleasure in helping you enjoy yourself to the max. As for the food, there is a daily choice of a delicious local or Western starter and main course, followed by an indulgent dessert.

The really good news is that Silolona has expanded her horizons. When I first discovered her, she was plying the seas between Amanwana and Komodo National Park, a sort of modern-day lost world with attendant 11-ft dragons; it has to be said this was one of my all time favourite two-center holidays. Now not only has she widened her reach to include more of the very best dive and snorkelling spots on earth, in places such as the Mergui Archipelago in Myanmar and Raja Ampat in West Papua, but also there is even the rumour of sister ships to follow. Simply put, these areas are generally accepted to offer some of the best diving in the world and Silolona is the best way to visit them. Select your destination and then the choice is yours whether to dive, snorkel or explore. What more needs to be said?

Komodo National Park has some of the best diving in the world, with over 1,200 species of fish and 250 types of coral – and new ones are still being discovered. The sheer biodiversity is amazing and virtually anything can be found in these waters, from the rare mimic octopus to warm-water killer whales. The quantity of marine life is staggering, and much of it is remarkably unafraid of divers.

DIVING

Komodo is both a national park and a national marine park, and its status is enforced despite the locals' fondness for dynamite fishing, so the reefs are truly flourishing. Some are covered in acres of immaculate staghorns; blizzards of fish rise and fall in time with your air bubbles, while inquisitive turtles seek you out.

The marine park has two very different areas, north and south, and the *Silolona* cruises both, depending on the season. The north provides warm-water diving, with endless visibility and clear turquoise waters. As you sail south, in a matter of a few miles, the water temperature drops from a balmy 30°C (86°F) to a numbing 19°C (66°F), and swells of plankton create a drop in visibility. Komodo is where the Indian and Pacific Oceans meet, and it is this constant welling-up of cold, nutrient-rich waters, especially from the Antarctic, that brings such a variety of life. It is crucial that you are accompanied by a highly experienced guide as the strong currents can be dangerous. The *Silolona*'s instructors more than qualify.

Two dives deserve special mention, and provided your timing is right, they simply have to be experienced. The first is Tatawa Besar, a pristine, seemingly endless reef festooned with both hard and soft corals, and fronted by a small white-sand beach that is perfect for

at a glance

Level	Easy to advanced (experience required for some of the best dives)
Visibility	100 ft+
Must-dives	Tatawa Besar, Tatawa Kecil, Gili Lawa Laut, Cannibal Rock, Ikelite Reef, Highway to Heaven, Castle Rock
Snorkelling	Superb
Wetsuits	3mm in north, 5mm in south
Coral	Superb
Marine life	Frogfish, leafish, nudibranchs, manta ray, whale shark, grey reef shark, schooling trevally, ghost pipefish, pygmy seahorse, killer whale, bumphead parrotfish, bobtail squid, mimic octopus
Other	Night dives, marine park, hyperbaric chamber in Bali (2 hrs)

lunch afterwards. Be sure to take a flashlight to bring out the amazing colours, particularly of the soft corals. There is so much to see that there is no point listing what you can expect to find.

The second dive is Tatawa Kecil, and while there are no colourful soft corals, it does reward you with blizzards of small fish exploding and retreating out of fields of staghorn. There are also bigger species including manta ray; look out for the rarer, even more striking black manta ray, which sometimes feed here. While the plankton means that visibility is far from perfect, it is this that brings in life as diverse as tuna, wahoo, bumphead parrotfish, giant wrasse, whale shark and shark. Another reason for the plethora of activity is that this small pinnacle is swept by fast currents, and currents bring predators. One end of the site is swept by powerful forces, but the other can be dived with relative ease; when the current becomes noticeable, you simply reverse the dive. Once again, your instructor's skill is essential, as without it some of these dives would be dangerous.

Komodo's underwater seascape is absolutely stunning, offering outstanding variety. It may be one of the planet's most sought-after dive destinations, but you don't have to be a diver to enjoy it. Snorkellers will be spoilt with some of the best sites in Indonesia, while those who stay above water will have an equally amazing time. There is truly something for everyone, from tranquil bays for snorkellers to mask-wrenching drift dives for seasoned thrill-seekers, from spine-tingling encounters with Komodo dragons to lazy days ending in beautiful sunsets. To be able to experience all this from such a unique and stylish boat makes it hard to beat. It's the ultimate way to visit this lost world.

The location could not be more exotic, hanging like an earring off the southern tip of Sulawesi in the Banda Sea. To make it easier and also to give you a great two-center holiday, you have to route through Bali, not exactly a hardship and a wonderful excuse to stay at one of the incomparable Aman resorts en route, specifically Amankila, which is the only place I know of where you can experience almost guaranteed encounters with the giant mola mola or sunfish.

sulawesi

HOTEL wakatobi dive resort

You can take in Bali either before or after, but I would suggest getting straight out to Wakatobi which offers seven- or ten-day trips, the inflexibility due to the private 90-minute charter from Bali, since there is no scheduled service. Touchdown is in the middle of nowhere and then finally onto your last leg to the island, a 15-minute boat ride.

Wakatobi resort was established on Onemobaa in 1995. It began as a simple dive resort with a determined eco-conscious status and accessibility that would have even put off Livingstone. It was a determined search by one man to find the ultimate location for a dive resort, and if you want the greatest biodiversity on the planet you head straight for Indonesia. With diving moving up market, so has the Wakatobi and now it almost qualifies as a boutique hotel in its own right. Of all the resorts in this book, this is the closest to a dive resort – there are no real children's facilities and not much to do aside from enjoying the pristine water and the environment.

The principal buildings and virtually all the rooms are perched right on the perfect white-sand beach. The original longhouse, formerly the entire resort, anchors the resort and now only houses the small spa, boutique and dive center. There are just 26 rooms in varying

at a glance

Airport	Bali
Airlines	British Airways, Singapore Airlines, Garuda, Thai Airways, Cathay Pacific Airways, Qatar
Transfer time	2 hrs, 30 mins private charter, 10 mins by bus, 15 mins by boat
Rooms	22 and 4 villas (all air-conditioned)
Staff ratio	3+
Activities	Kayaking, paddle boarding, island tours, ping pong, volleyball
Services	Wi-fi, small spa, boutique
Children	Any age, babysitters available
Power type	UK 3-pin (adaptors available)
Currency	US dollar
GMT	+8
Booking	www.diveinstyle.com

categories, giving you four budget-dependent choices ranging from garden bungalows all the way up to the four new villas, which really set themselves apart, literally and figuratively, and, dependent on budget, this is where you should head. The new villas are constructed on a rocky cliff perched a few feet above the sea, accessed via a short stairway and with direct sea access. With private plunge pool, large bathrooms, covered decks and private sun decks, they are simply the best rooms I believe you will find at any pure dive resort anywhere.

The rooms, all now air-conditioned, are set right on the beach or the garden behind, all planted in the sand until you climb the stone and concrete path to the villas. You will not see this in any report, but the concentration of marine life here is such that it literally overflows the ocean: don't be surprised to find slothful sea snakes collapsed in a heap on the sand at night.

A short stroll from anywhere is the soaring dining pavilion fronting directly onto the beach and, again, given how remote you are, the food is excellent. Breakfast can be served in your room, but all other meals are served in the restaurant. Quite often you will find yourself sharing a table, but if you crave privacy, then either ask for your own table or enjoy a privately catered dinner on the beach. Either way, a stop at the jetty bar, perched over the clear waters, is a good starting point.

Wakatobi is something of an enigma, straddling the divide between luxury dive resorts and boutique hotels. The atmosphere is incredibly relaxed, the local staff ever helpful, and given where you are it is an amazing achievement, the more so as it puts so much back into the local community. Without the hotel's existence, it is frighteningly credible that the reefs would by now have been dynamited to extinction.

Now occupying what used to be the entire hotel, it is at the spacious open-sided longhouse that you gather before nearly every dive for your briefing. On arrival you are allocated one of the dive boats, Wakatobi 1 to 8, and it is yours for the duration. The system could not be easier: just check the board as you leave the dining room to find out where and when the briefing is and manage the three-minute stroll to the dive center – your gear will have beaten you to the boat.

DIVE CENTER

You can even have your own instructor, if you want. Regardless, everyone gets to share the post-dive drinks, coconut and freshly baked biscuits. It may be that you don't feel like joining the boat, so you can simply dive the house reef, solo. Just ask and you will be dropped off at the perfect spot, allowing for the current and you can just drift along what has to be the world's best house reef, just the two of you, the exit points being clearly marked. This normally deposits you in the shallows just off the dining room where, as if by magic, the staff appear to relieve you of your bottles. Sensational and repeatable and if you have never dived on your own before, this is the place to start – you simply cannot get lost and this is a must-dive.

If the resort is not enough, then book a berth on board their luxury live-aboard, the 100-ft *Pelagian* which will take you to more distant reefs. Either way you will not be disappointed.

at a glance

Boats	60 ft, dry, covered (100-ft *Pelagian* live-aboard)
Group size	4 (private guides available)
Instructors	15
Languages	English
Courses	Mostly nitrox, advanced and technical
Children	12+
Other	Computer hire, camera rooms, gear prep and wash down, nitrox, private dive guides, night dives

Where to start? How about 400 species of coral and 700 species of fish officially recorded, not in Indonesia generally, but here in Wakatobi. A further statistic, a yardstick used by marine biologists to establish the health and diversity of the reef, is the number of species of butterflyfish encountered. The highest count I can find is 40, and that is here in Wakatobi. That's probably all I need to say, however...

RIGHT
A mantis shrimp guards its lair and, armed with a club that has the power of a .22 rifle, is well equipped to do so.

ABOVE
This map pufferfish is about the largest fish you will find on these reefs.

RIGHT
Beautiful clownfish of many species adorn every anemone.

DIVING

The majority of dives take place on either the fringing reef of neighbouring Lintea Island or even closer to home. With crystalline water, visibility can be up to 150 ft. I can still recall the reef shallows and clear depths just calling me to get in the water for my first dive. Aside from anything else, most of the dives are incredibly gentle, normally a slow drift dive and here I have one criticism. The boats do follow you very carefully, but being picky, the constant thrum of their engines is at odds with the pristine beauty of the underwater environment.

Frankly, no dive really stands out, you just have to get used to pouring over the reefs searching for some of the exotic marine life that calls Wakatobi home. If you are after big life, Wakatobi is not really for you: I think I saw one shark, some pristine turtles, bumphead parrotfish and two eagle rays, however, maybe one is so fixated on the reef that frankly a pod of whales could have swum behind me and I wouldn't have noticed.

Your guides need to be, and indeed are, underwater bushmen, evidenced by the first time you see such life as the robust ghost pipefish. Even though your guide puts his finger a few inches away, pointing, you are convinced you are looking at a leaf until your mind begins to understand that it is actually alive. The more easily recognizable and stunningly beautiful ornate ghost pipefish is also not in short supply.

ABOVE
The stunning and delicate ghost pipefish in an unusual shade of green.

RIGHT
Soft corals of every hue resemble a flower stall.

at a glance

Local sites	40+
Level	Easy–advanced
Visibility	100 ft
Must-dives	All of them
Snorkelling	Excellent on house reef, superb from dive boat. Try mangrove snorkelling at high tide
Wetsuits	3mm
Coral	Pristine, hard and soft
Marine life	Eagle ray, bumphead parrotfish, blue ribbon eels, leaffish, crocodilefish, endless nudibranchs, mandarinfish, frogfish, pygmy seahorse, mantis shrimp, pygmy squid, blue ringed octopus, pilot whales
Other	Hyperbaric chamber on Bali, night dives

LEFT
Crocodilefish are literally
two a penny.

OPPOSITE, ABOVE, LEFT
An exquisite, ornate ghost
pipefish.

OPPOSITE, ABOVE,
RIGHT
Moving like its name, the
leaf ghost pipefish is at first
impossible to differentiate
from pieces of weed.

OPPOSITE, BELOW
What can you say about
corals like this – and there
are miles of them.

LEFT
Blue ribbon eels on demand.

BELOW, LEFT
Endless colourful
nudibranchs in stunning
livery.

OPPOSITE, CLOCKWISE
FROM TOP LEFT
Possibly the most beautiful
fish in the sea, the vividly
coloured mandarinfish;
scorpionfish are everywhere
and nearly impossible to
see and thus act as a good
encouragement not to touch
the reef; a gobi peers from
his hole; a slipper lobster.

One of the most sought-after of marine life must surely be the pygmy
seahorse, and here they are in abundance, the difficulty is in seeing
them either with the naked eye or even through a camera lens, unless
you have really good equipment. Some are literally the size of a grain
of rice, the exact same colour as the fan they call home and thus virtually
invisible. With no eyelids, they suffer only a few strobe flashes before
hurrying away into open water, which can mean to their death, so due
consideration should be given to these wonderful creatures.

Nudibranchs of every variety abound, clownfish of every type
and size including some huge cartoon-like specimens. All the
traditional residents are also in abundance, whether leaf scorpionfish,
scorpionfish, crocodilefish, schools of marauding bumphead
parrotfish, blue ribbon eels, it just goes on. The end of virtually every
dive is spent at the five-metre mark just drinking in the incredible
corals, transparent water and endless life, all lit to perfection.

There is not enough space to describe all the sites here and given
the locals knowledge, you can just sit back knowing that wherever
you dive will reward.

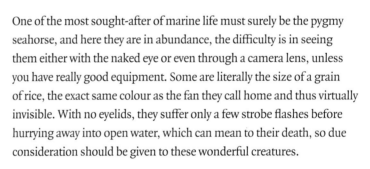

POSITE, CLOCKWISE
OM TOP LEFT

blue ribbon eel is
ally a transsexual,
nging sex along with
ur; the photographer's
grail – about the
of a grain of rice and
ossible to distinguish
n its habitat, without
t, one of a number of
cies of pygmy seahorse
s one is pregnant);
uid blends perfectly
the colourful coral;
another stunning
branch.

Average high
Average low
Water temperature
Rainfall

australia

Seasons are the reverse of the northern hemisphere – summer is winter and winter, summer. The figures below are for Cairns, and Lizard Island is normally drier. Don't go here especially to see whales or mantas as they are unreliable; just go, as the coral is still incredible.

	Jan	Feb	Mar	Apr	May	Jun	Jul	Aug	Sep	Oct	Nov	Dec
High	31°	31°	31°	29°	28°	26°	26°	27°	28°	29°	31°	31°
Low	24	24	23	22	20	18°	17	17	19°	21	24	20
Water	29°	27°	27°	27°	26°	26°	22°	22°	23°	26°	27°	28°
Rainfall	277mm	285mm	183mm	84mm	33mm	36mm	15mm	13mm	18mm	33mm	49mm	130mm

Best for diving

Minke & humpback whale

Manta

fiji

Being south of the Equator, the seasons are the reverse of the northern hemisphere, and December to April is the rainy season. The rainfall figures are for the mainland; the outlying islands, such as Wakaya and Vatulele, receive less rain.

	Jan	Feb	Mar	Apr	May	Jun	Jul	Aug	Sep	Oct	Nov	Dec
High	30°	30°	29°	29°	28°	27°	27°	27°	28°	28°	29°	31°
Low	23	23	23	22	22	21	20	20	20	20	22	23
Water	28°	28°	29°	29°	28°	27°	26°	25°	25°	25°	26°	27°
Rainfall	280mm	280mm	355mm	304mm	254mm	165mm	127mm	203mm	203mm	215mm	254mm	304mm

Best for diving

french polynesia

Forget celebrating Christmas here if you want sunshine. These islands are beautiful and lush for a reason. The figures are for Bora Bora and the Society Islands; Tikehau does have less rain.

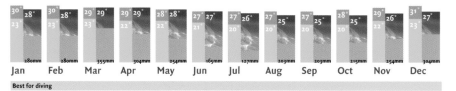

	Jan	Feb	Mar	Apr	May	Jun	Jul	Aug	Sep	Oct	Nov	Dec
High	32°	32°	32°	31°	31°	30°	30°	30°	30°	31°	31°	32°
Low	22	22	22	22	22	21	21	21	21	21	22	22
Water	29°	29°	28°	27°	27°	26°	26°	26°	26°	28°	28°	29°
Rainfall	250mm	240mm	430mm	140mm	100mm	76mm	50mm	38mm	50mm	90mm	150mm	254mm

Best for diving

Manta and eagle ray

Hammerhead (Tikehau only)

Humpback whale

costa rica

May to November is rainy season (normally sunny in the morning and some rain in the afternoon) but the seas are calm, and it is the best time for the Catalina and Bat Islands. The best visibility is in the dry season, December through April.

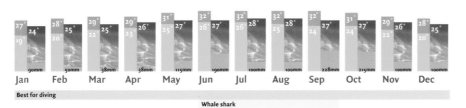

	Jan	Feb	Mar	Apr	May	Jun	Jul	Aug	Sep	Oct	Nov	Dec
High	32°	33°	33°	33°	32°	31°	31°	31°	31°	30°	30°	31°
Low	24°	25°	25°	25°	25°	25°	25°	24°	24°	24°	24°	24°
Sea	21°	22°	23°	24°	25°	27°	28°	28°	29°	28°	25°	24°
Rain	8mm	3mm	5mm	33mm	200mm	240mm	183mm	244mm	310mm	254mm	120mm	33mm

Best for diving
Cow rays schooling
Manta   Pilot whale
Whale shark
Humpback whale
                        Killer whale

---

mexico

While the weather is normally settled, remember that August to November is hurricane season. Although this is unlikely to disrupt your holiday, it should be borne in mind.

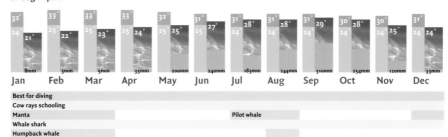

	Jan	Feb	Mar	Apr	May	Jun	Jul	Aug	Sep	Oct	Nov	Dec
High	27°	28°	29°	29°	31°	32°	32°	32°	32°	31°	29°	28°
Low	24°	25°	25°	26°	27°	27°	28°	28°	27°	27°	26°	25°
Sea	19°	20°	22°	23°	25°	26°	26°	25°	27°	24°	22°	20°
Rain	90mm	50mm	38mm	38mm	115mm	190mm	100mm	100mm	228mm	215mm	100mm	100mm

Best for diving
                        Whale shark

---

usa

Beware the almost traditional Florida 'cold snap' around the New Year.

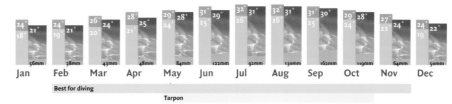

	Jan	Feb	Mar	Apr	May	Jun	Jul	Aug	Sep	Oct	Nov	Dec
High	24°	24°	26°	28°	29°	31°	32°	32°	31°	29°	27°	24°
Low	21°	21°	24°	25°	28°	29°	31°	31°	30°	28°	24°	22°
Sea	18°	19°	20°	21°	24°	26°	26°	26°	25°	24°	22°	19°
Rain	56mm	38mm	43mm	48mm	84mm	122mm	92mm	130mm	162mm	119mm	64mm	50mm

Best for diving
                        Tarpon

---

belize

This subtropical climate has a mean humidity of 83 per cent but is usually comfortable thanks to the cooling winds. Diving is great all year round, but for a guaranteed thrill, whale shark season cannot be beaten for divers and snorkellers alike.

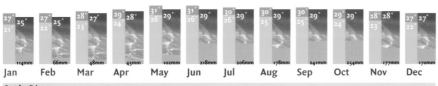

	Jan	Feb	Mar	Apr	May	Jun	Jul	Aug	Sep	Oct	Nov	Dec
High	27°	27°	28°	29°	31°	31°	30°	30°	30°	29°	28°	27°
Low	25°	25°	27°	28°	29°	29°	29°	29°	29°	29°	28°	27°
Sea	21°	22°	23°	24°	26°	26°	26°	25°	25°	24°	23°	22°
Rain	114mm	66mm	48mm	43mm	102mm	218mm	206mm	178mm	241mm	254mm	177mm	170mm

Best for diving
Grouper spawning
                Whale shark
                        Loggerhead turtle
        Manta (Glovers Reef)
        Mating manatees

caribbean

August and September can be hot and still as it is hurricane season. If you're whale-watching on the *Aggressor*, take a fleece and a lightweight waterproof jacket, and note that the last trip ends at Grand Turk, a short hop from Amanyara in the Turks and Caicos.

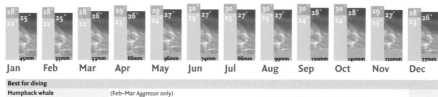

	Jan	Feb	Mar	Apr	May	Jun	Jul	Aug	Sep	Oct	Nov	Dec
high	28°	28°	28°	29°	29°	30°	30°	30°	30°	30°	29°	28°
	25°	25°	26°	26°	27°	27°	27°	27°	28°	28°	27°	26°
low	22	22	22	23	24	25	25	25	24	24	23	23
rain	45mm	35mm	53mm	66mm	96mm	74mm	66mm	99mm	120mm	140mm	120mm	77mm

Best for diving
Humpback whale (Feb–Mar *Aggressor* only)
Tarpon and jack schools

italy

The busy season runs from 25 June to 28 August, so book early. September offers the best compromise: the waters are warm and the August rush is over.

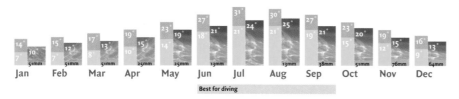

	Jan	Feb	Mar	Apr	May	Jun	Jul	Aug	Sep	Oct	Nov	Dec
high	14°	15°	17°	19°	23°	27°	31°	30°	27°	23°	19°	16°
	10°	12°	13°	15°	19°	21°	24°	25°	21°	20°	15°	13°
low	7	7	8	10	14	18	21	21	19	15	12	9
rain	51mm	51mm	51mm	25mm	25mm	13mm	13mm	38mm	51mm	76mm	64mm	

Best for diving

egypt

If you want guaranteed sunshine, just look at the rainfall figures! It gets hot in summer but if you can bear it, this is when the fish and shark can form huge schools and the diving is at its zenith.

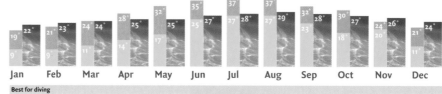

	Jan	Feb	Mar	Apr	May	Jun	Jul	Aug	Sep	Oct	Nov	Dec
high	19°	21°	24°	28°	32°	35°	37°	37°	32°	30°	24°	21°
	22°	23°	24°	25°		25° 27°	27° 28°	27° 29°	28°	27°	26°	24°
low	9	9	11	14	17	25			23	18	20	11

Best for diving
Schooling hammerhead
Schooling fish
Silky shark

oman

Oman is generally humid but especially so during the summer months when it is HOT. It's probably best to avoid Ramadan as there are various dining restrictions which will mean you will mostly eat indoors.

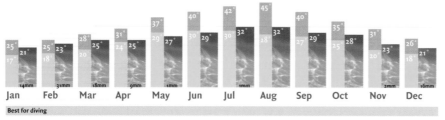

	Jan	Feb	Mar	Apr	May	Jun	Jul	Aug	Sep	Oct	Nov	Dec
high	25°	25°	28°	31°	37°	40°	42°	45°	40°	35°	31°	26°
	21°	23°	25°	29° 27°	30° 29°	30° 32°	32°	28°	27° 29°	25° 28°	23°	21°
low	17	18	20	24 25							18	
rain	14mm	31mm	18mm	9mm			1mm			2mm	16mm	

Best for diving

tanzania

Late March to late May is the long rainy season and considered winter. Check the tides with the resort before you book.

	Jan	Feb	Mar	Apr	May	Jun	Jul	Aug	Sep	Oct	Nov	Dec
High °C	31	31	32	31	29	29	29	29	29	30	31	31
Low °C	25	24	24	24	22	20	19	19	20	20	23	23
Water °C	27	27	28	27	27	25	25	25	25	25	26	26
Rainfall	50mm	50mm	76mm	127mm	152mm	25mm	25mm	25mm	25mm	25mm	50mm	50mm

Best for diving — resort closed mid-April to mid-June

Turtle hatching

Humpback whale

mozambique

Avoid February and March when the rain can last for days at a time. Manta and whale shark are only found at Marlin.

	Jan	Feb	Mar	Apr	May	Jun	Jul	Aug	Sep	Oct	Nov	Dec
High °C	31	31	31	28	26	26	26	26	26	24	28	31
Low °C	22	22	21	18	16	13	13	14	16	18	18	18
Water °C	28	28	28	26	25	22	22	22	24	25	26	26
Rainfall	125mm	120mm	120mm	50mm	25mm	18mm	10mm	10mm	25mm	50mm	8mm	100mm

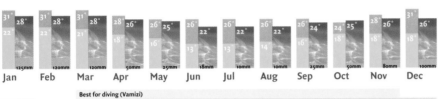

Best for diving (Vamizi)

Best for diving (Marlin Lodge)

Manta

Whale shark

Green turtle laying eggs

Humpback whales

seychelles

Being close to the Equator, air and water temperatures vary little. The more humid rainy season runs from November to April, and the downpours, when they come, can be heavy, but last only a short while before the sunshine returns. Avoid July and August for diving. For whale shark, it's best to stay on Mahé.

	Jan	Feb	Mar	Apr	May	Jun	Jul	Aug	Sep	Oct	Nov	Dec
High °C	28	29	29	30	29	28	28	27	28	28	28	28
Low °C	24	25	25	25	25	24	24	24	24	24	24	24
Water °C	27	28	29	30	29	26	26	27	27	28	28	27
Rainfall	380mm	254mm	228mm	178mm	178mm	100mm	100mm	76mm	127mm	152mm	228mm	330mm

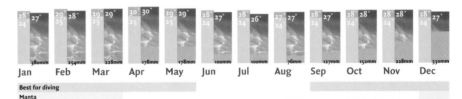

Best for diving

Manta

Whale shark

maldives

There are two seasons: the wet season from May to November, which brings mantas but has worse visibility, and the dry season from December to April, when visibility is much better (best for photos), the currents stronger, and there are more shark and eagle ray. Low season is still good weather and great diving.

	Jan	Feb	Mar	Apr	May	Jun	Jul	Aug	Sep	Oct	Nov	Dec
High °C	29	29	29	31	31	31	30	30	30	29	29	29
Low °C	23	24	25	27	26	24	24	25	24	24	23	23
Water °C	29	30	30	29	28	27	27	28	28	28	29	29
Rainfall	50mm	25mm	25mm	50mm	178mm	304mm	228mm	203mm	152mm	178mm	127mm	76mm

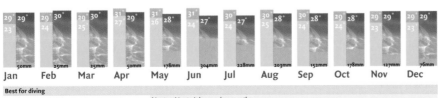

Best for diving

Manta – May to July are prime months

Whale shark

thailand

Avoid the turn of the seasons in October and May. If you especially want to dive the Similans, November to April is the time to do it as they are closed the rest of the year. For the best visibility, try and avoid the new moon; half-moon diving is best. If you're looking for whale shark and manta then head to Hin Deang and Hin Muang – a long day trip.

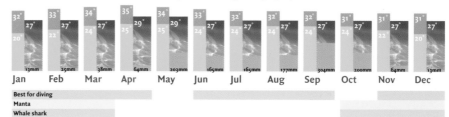

	Jan	Feb	Mar	Apr	May	Jun	Jul	Aug	Sep	Oct	Nov	Dec
Air high	32°	33°	34°	35°	34°	33°	32°	32°	32°	31°	31°	31°
Water	27°	27°	27°	29°	29°	27°	27°	27°	27°	27°	27°	27°
Air low	20°	22°	24°		25°	24°	24°	24°	24°	24°	22°	20°
Rainfall	13mm	25mm	38mm	64mm	203mm	165mm	165mm	177mm	304mm	200mm	64mm	13mm

Best for diving
Manta
Whale shark

---

philippines

The best and calmest conditions are from March to May, when you can dive most sites, although it is good all year round with at least one of Pamalican's coasts always being accessible to dive.

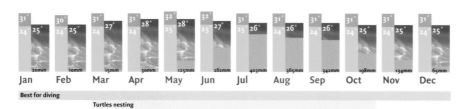

	Jan	Feb	Mar	Apr	May	Jun	Jul	Aug	Sep	Oct	Nov	Dec
Air high	31°	30°	31°	31°	32°	32°	31°	31°	31°	31°	31°	31°
Water	25°	25°	27°	28°	28°	27°	26°	26°	26°	25°	25°	25°
Air low	24°	24°	24°	24°	25°	25°	25°	24°	24°	24°	24°	24°
Rainfall	20mm	10mm	15mm	30mm	125mm	262mm	403mm	365mm	342mm	198mm	134mm	65mm

Best for diving
Turtles nesting

---

indonesia

Avoid the rainy season between January and March. Diving is always fantastic but it is at its very best between April and October. The figures are for Moyo and north Komodo, whereas the water can be up to 8 degrees colder in south Komodo.

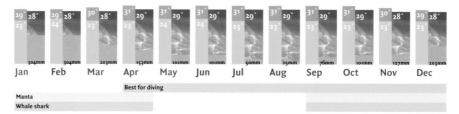

	Jan	Feb	Mar	Apr	May	Jun	Jul	Aug	Sep	Oct	Nov	Dec
Air high	29°	29°	30°	31°	31°	31°	31°	31°	31°	31°	30°	29°
Water	28°	28°	28°	29°	29°	29°	29°	29°	29°	29°	28°	28°
Air low	23°	24°	23°	23°	24°	23°	23°	23°	23°	23°	23°	23°
Rainfall	304mm	304mm	203mm	153mm	101mm	101mm	50mm	25mm	76mm	101mm	127mm	203mm

Best for diving
Manta
Whale shark

Wakatobi experiences marked less rainfall than Moyo and thus is generally drier with less humidity. April, May, October and November are hot with little wind whereas January, February, July and August are cooler with breeze. Most rain occurs from December to February but mostly just a few hours here and there. Consequently diving is great all year round.

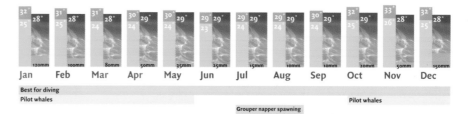

	Jan	Feb	Mar	Apr	May	Jun	Jul	Aug	Sep	Oct	Nov	Dec
Air high	32°	31°	31°	30°	30°	29°	29°	29°	30°	32°	33°	32°
Water	28°	28°	28°	29°	29°	29°	29°	29°	29°	29°	28°	28°
Air low	25°	25°	25°	24°	24°	23°	24°	24°	24°	25°	26°	25°
Rainfall	120mm	100mm	80mm	50mm	35mm	25mm	15mm	10mm	10mm	20mm	50mm	150mm

Best for diving
Pilot whales   **Pilot whales**
Grouper napper spawning

diving terms

Atoll
A low-lying coral island, often with wonderful white sand.

Barrier reef
A large reef system, normally some miles from the shore, forming a 'barrier' at sea level and protecting the coastline from the open ocean.

BC/BCD
Buoyancy Control Device – a jacket worn by divers to adjust their buoyancy

Bleaching
Under conditions of extreme stress (usually but not exclusively caused by global phenomena such as El Niño), coral is forced to expel the single-celled algae that live inside it and provide its colour. The coral then dies, and acquires a white or bleached appearance.

Bommie
A free-standing coral 'hill' that rises from the sea bed but does not form part of a reef.

DAN
Divers Alert Network is a non-profit organization dedicated to the safety and health of recreational scuba divers. DAN medical insurance is a very cost-effective way of ensuring full medical back-up in the event of a diving accident. Highly recommended.

Dive computer
A wrist or console-mounted gauge that monitors all elements of your dive and indicates your nitrogen absorption and when you must move to shallower waters – an important tool in avoiding decompression sickness.

Drift dive
A dive where the boat follows you as you 'drift' along in the current in one direction, as opposed to swimming in one direction and then reversing course to return to the moored boat.

Live-aboard
A small 'cruise' boat, normally providing cabins for around 25 guests, which takes you to the more distant and inaccessible reefs and becomes a floating hotel to dive from.

Nitrox
As opposed to compressed air normally breathed, nitrox is a blend richer in oxygen and with less nitrogen, enabling longer dives at certain depths. To dive nitrox you need to be qualified in its use.

Open-water certificate
The qualification needed to become a certified diver.

Pelagic
Marine life of the open ocean, such as shark and manta ray, rather than reef-dwelling species.

Rebreather
Equipment that enables you to dive without producing bubbles or sound; consequently, marine life treats you as one of them. Specialist training required.

Reef hook
A hook on a cord which you clip onto dead reef to enable you to float in one position in a current. Only used in Palau in this book.

Refresher course
If you are a qualified diver but have not dived for some time, this simple course will remind you of the basics.

Regulator
The mouthpiece through which you breath and which regulates the supply of air.

Resort course
A short course to introduce you to the world of scuba and enable you to enjoy the thrill without having to be qualified. Depth and conditions limited.

RIB
A boat with a rigid hull surrounded by a large Zodiac-like rubber tube.

SCUBA
Self-Contained Underwater Breathing Apparatus, originally invented by Jacques Cousteau and Emile Gagnan in 1942, by cannibalizing a demand valve from a WWII gas-powered Citroën.

Soft in-water encounter
A very gentle encounter where the animal is happy to interact with humans on its own terms.

Wall dive
As opposed to floating over coral or a sandy bottom, here you have the thrill of diving off 'the wall'. This will be on one shoulder and is normally an almost vertical drop into deep blue. Here you have the best chance of seeing the larger pelagic life. Many of the best dives are wall dives as you fly along over the abyss, a fabulous experience.

Throughout this book, the 'at a glance' columns provide an immediate overview of key facts about the hotels, dive centers and diving. Below is some more general information about the less obvious headings.

Hotel at a glance

Airport	The nearest main airport to the resort.
Airlines	The principal airlines that service the main airport.
Staff ratio	The ratio of staff per room. As a rule of thumb, the higher the number, the more you will be pampered.
Services	Mobile phones: Whether or not most cellphones have reception at the resort, and whether the resort permits them at all in deference to other guests.
Children	The minimum age from which the hotel accepts children.
Power type	Most of the hotels featured have adaptors available, but there is always a chance that they are already being used by other guests. This guide should help you find the adaptor you require. For more details, see www.kropla.com
Booking	The Dive in Style website (www.diveinstyle.com) provides a link to Original Travel, a specialist travel agency with whom I have worked closely to select these resorts. You can also contact them directly through their website (www.originaltravel.co.uk) or +44 (0)20 7978 7333. Their team is familiar with all the destinations in this book and will tailor everything for your holiday including flights, hotel reservations, transfers, diving and any extensions you may want to add to your trip, as well as offering expert advice. Alternatively, contact details for the hotels are listed if you wish to book direct.

Dive Center at a glance

When selecting hotels, I have tried to ensure that all the resorts have convenient in-house dive centers equipped with a high standard of equipment so that you will not need to take anything with you. However, I would always suggest that you travel with your own mask and where possible, dive computer, since not all centers have computers for hire.

Boats	The minimum size of boat available. 26 ft+ means there is more than one boat, with the smallest being 26 ft. 30 ft without the + means just one 30-ft boat.
	Covered/Open: Whether the boats have shade or not.
	Wet/Dry: Is there adequate protection from rain or sea (and a place to store cameras, etc.), or is it a 'wet boat'?
Group size	The largest group that you will dive in, excluding the instructor, although the average size can often be smaller.
Languages	The languages spoken by the dive staff are important if you are thinking of learning at that resort.
Courses	PADI (www.padi.com) is the world's largest diving association and the most recognized series of dive qualifications worldwide. Through associated dive centers who offer a range of courses, their training will ensure you are introduced to the underwater world in safe hands.
Children	Not all resorts have gear suitable for children; this will tell you the age they cater from. While Bubblemaker courses are available from age 8, and junior open water from age 10, many centers (and I agree) prefer to add two years to these minimum ages.
Other	Wash down: The dive center will look after your gear and rinse it at the end of each dive so you have no responsibility except to turn up to dive.
	Drinks: Whether water or even food is provided on board.
	Computer hire: If not mentioned, it is not provided, so you might like to consider bringing your own.
	Private charters: This means that private charters are available as an option.

Diving at a glance

Local sites	The number of convenient dive sites within 30 minutes.
Level	The degree of difficulty of the dives. All the resorts I have selected are suitable for novice or beginner divers, although some of the more thrilling dives, such as drift dives, may require more experience.
Visibility	This is an average but will vary according to the season.
Must-dives	Recommended sites.
Snorkelling	The house reef is right off the hotel beach. Sometimes you are able to join the dive boat on its trips to the reefs and snorkel in shallower areas where they exist.
Wetsuits	The colder the water, the thicker the wetsuit you require. For most of the regions visited, 3mm is generally adequate with one or two exceptions, depending upon the season.
Marine life	This is not an exhaustive list, but simply the more unusual or sought-after sea life you might see.
Other	Hyperbaric chamber: Required for recompression treatment in the unlikely event of decompression sickness (the bends).
	Marine park: An area in which the marine life is protected by law, and so tends to be more relaxed and plentiful.